Sanctification in the New Testament

SANCTIFICATION
in the New Testament

by
Ralph Earle

Beacon Hill Press of Kansas City
Kansas City, Missouri

Contents

Foreword

Ralph Earle, a scholar known and read throughout world Christianity, is really at heart a gospel preacher of depth and simplicity. This comes through beautifully in this latest book, *Sanctification in the New Testament*. A lifetime in the classroom has served to spur him on to explain with great clarity and effectiveness the work of the Holy Spirit in practical terms. During those years in the classroom he balanced his ministry with consistent pulpit work in camp meetings, revivals, and conventions. His heartbeat then and now is that people will see the light and press on to the glorious fulfillment of the experience of holiness.

His impressive record of scholarly achievements can be found elsewhere, but he leaves a record of writings, translations, and practical helps that will continue to instruct and bless the followers of Christ for many decades to come.

Sanctification in the New Testament lifts up some of the outstanding biblical passages on holiness from which Dr. Earle draws spiritual holiness lessons. How to have a holy church or a holy life is a subject for intense scrutiny.

This small book is the essence of practical, biblical holiness compressed into a few simply-stated chapters. Every page is filled with meaning easily understood by the reader. As he has done in hundreds of camp meetings and local church revivals, Dr. Earle explains the way more perfectly.

RAYMOND W. HURN

Preface

In the spring of 1986 I was asked to teach three weeks at the Seminario Nazareno Mexicano, outside Mexico City. I suggested to Dr. Honorato Reza, the founding president, that I might give a course on "Sanctification in Paul's Epistles." Then I recalled that in 1940 I wrote my doctoral dissertation in Boston on "The Doctrine of Sanctification in the New Testament." So I broadened the subject of my seminary course to "Sanctification in the New Testament," the title of this book.

At the end of the second week, as we came to the close of the last session on Friday, I sensed that the Holy Spirit was moving in the hearts of some of the students. Asking them all to close their eyes, I said, "Is there someone here who feels that you need to be sanctified?"

Several hands were raised. We went to our knees in prayer, and soon five students prayed through to clear victory. In the classroom I had not only delineated the doctrine but also emphasized the experience.

Finally came the last session of the course. As it was about time to dismiss the class at twelve o'clock, a student raised his hand and asked for permission to speak. Then he stood to his feet and with vibrant voice declared: "This has been the greatest week of my life, since I was sanctified last Friday noon!" The other four who had prayed followed him with equally joyous testimonies. Then the whole class formed a circle around the room and sang several songs of thanksgiving to God. The atmosphere was electrified with the Holy Spirit's presence.

My main field of teaching over a period of 50 years (1933-83) has been New Testament, in Greek and English. Exegesis and exposition, in the classroom and pulpit, has been my vocation. In the latter place it has always ended with application and exhortation.

This book is not a theological treatise. My primary purpose and deep concern has been to help people see the light of this glorious truth of entire sanctification and receive this gracious experience.

During many years of intensive study of the Greek text I have become increasingly convinced that the New Testament teaches entire sanctification as a second crisis in Christian experience. This is God's will (1 Thess. 4:3) for every born-again believer.

Back in the 18th century John Wesley was concerned about people failing to walk in the light of holiness. He wrote:

> I am not afraid that the people called Methodists should ever cease to exist either in Europe or America. But I am afraid, lest they should only exist as a dead sect, having the form of religion without the power. And this undoubtedly will be the case, unless they hold fast both the doctrine, spirit, and discipline with which they first set out. (*Works,* Thomas Jackson edition, 13:258)

Two hundred years later it has been acknowledged in England that there are more Muslims than Methodists in the land of the Wesleys. God forbid that a similar fate should overtake the holiness movement in the United States!

Shortly before Dr. J. B. Chapman died he was asked, "Do you think the day will ever come when the Church of the Nazarene will cease to teach and preach old-fashioned, second blessing holiness?"

His reply was, "No." But then, with tears streaming down his face, he added: "The thing I fear is that the time will come when our people will have the theory but not possess the experience." This is strikingly similar to what John Wesley said, as quoted above.

What was Dr. Chapman's own position on the subject of sanctification? In his book *Holiness, the Heart of Christian Experience* (p. 10) he wrote: "Regeneration and entire sanctification are the two crises in which God deals with the sin problem in us and by which He takes us out of sin and then takes sin out of us." That expresses the truth very clearly. He also declared: "We have the task of bringing the people of God into the grace and blessing of Bible sanctification" (*All Out for Souls,* 7).

1

MATTHEW

1. Baptism with the Holy Spirit (3:11)

Some years ago the Church of the Nazarene was holding a General Assembly in the Civic Auditorium in downtown Kansas City. When the general superintendent in charge of the session had been graciously welcomed by a city leader, he sought to enliven the situation with a facetious remark like this: "You know, we are the oldest Christian denomination in the world. We are the Church of the *Nazarene.*" Immediately the city leader stepped forward with the counterproposal: "I'm a Baptist. We are older than you because we go back to John the Baptist." Of course everybody laughed, and the assembly got off to a pleasant start.

What did John the Baptist preach? We are all familiar with his main message: "Repent, for the kingdom of heaven is near" (Matt. 3:2). And Jesus began His messianic ministry with exactly the same text (4:17).

But too often it is forgotten that John the Baptist went on to say: "I baptize you with water for repentance. But after me will come one who is more powerful than I . . . He will baptize you with the Holy Spirit and with fire" (Matt. 3:11)—that is, with a fiery, cleansing baptism with the Holy Spirit. This is what Jesus came to bring. Mrs. C. H. Morris put it well:

There is sanctifying power,
Like a sweet, refreshing shower,
  Waiting for each consecrated heart:
Power to cleanse us from all sin,
Power to keep us pure within,
  Power for service which He will impart.

Across nearly 2,000 years of Christian history the church has given consistent emphasis to the importance of water baptism. But how much preaching has there been on the fiery baptism of the Holy Spirit that will cleanse the heart from sin? That is one of the great needs of our day.

That fire was used as a cleansing agent is illustrated in Num. 31:22-23: "Gold, silver, bronze, iron, tin, lead and anything else that can withstand fire must be put through the fire, and then it will be clean." Only fire could destroy dangerous disease germs. And the worst disease in all the universe is sin in the human heart. The only way we can be cleansed from that disease is by the baptism with the Holy Spirit and fire. Let us resound that tremendous truth today.

2. The Pure in Heart (5:8)

The Sermon on the Mount begins with eight beatitudes. The sixth one is:

> "Blessed are the pure in heart,
>   for they will see God."

Who are "the pure in heart"? The great Danish philosopher Kierkegaard wrote: "Purity of heart is to will one intention." That is, the pure in heart have just one intent and desire, and that is to do the will of God. This can only be true when our hearts have been cleansed from all self-will. We no longer want our own way; we just want God's way. And only the fiery baptism of the Holy Spirit can "burn out the dross of inbred sin"—to use the words of a familiar song.

To the pure in heart the glorious promise is made: "For they will see God." This is often interpreted as meaning that after we leave this world we will see God. It also means that we will see Him here and now. Sin is like dust in the eyes; it beclouds our vision of God and distorts our view of Him. Only a fully cleansed heart can see God clearly.

3. The Cost of Discipleship (16:24)

Jesus said: "If anyone would come after me, he must deny himself and take up his cross and follow me."

What is self-denial? It is the opposite of self-assertion. If we are going to be Christ's disciples, we have to acknowledge that we cannot save ourselves; only He can save us. We cannot have our own way; we must let Him have His way.

And what does it mean to take up one's cross? Jesus has given us the example for this. In Gethsemane He prayed: "Not my will, but yours be done" (Luke 22:42). For Him it meant death on the Cross. And so cross-bearing means dying to self, going Jesus' way—the way of the Cross. It means saying to God: "Not my will, but yours be done."

In the Greek the verbs *deny* and *take up* are in the aorist tense, which suggests momentary action. But the verb *follow* is in the present tense of continuous action. So the verse may be taken as indicating two crises—a crucial conversion and a complete consecration—and then a continual following Christ the rest of our lives. That is the price we have to pay to be a true disciple of Jesus.

2

ACTS

1. Pentecost (1:5, 8; 2:1-11)

One of the great evangelists of the last generation was Gypsy Smith. Once he was asked: "What is the greatest need of the Church today?"

His immediate answer was: "Another Pentecost!"

The inquirer then asked: "What is the second greatest need?"

Once more the evangelist replied: "Another Pentecost!"

The questioner probed one more time by asking: "And what is the third most important need?"

Gypsy had just one answer to give: "Another Pentecost!"

We would heartily agree with his assessment. But what does "Pentecost" mean? That is what we want to investigate as we look into Acts.

Pentecost is the most important event in the Book of Acts. Without it the book would never have been written, for there would have been nothing to write.

Pentecost is the Greek word for "fifty." It is the New Testament name—adopted by the Jews in the intertestamental period—for the Old Testament "Feast of Weeks." Deut. 16:9-10 gives background: "Count off seven weeks from the time you begin to put the sickle to the standing grain. Then celebrate the Feast of Weeks to the Lord your God." After the 49-day interval, the feast took place on the 50th day. That was why it was called "Pentecost."

In Acts 1:4 Jesus told the disciples not to leave Jerusalem, "but wait for the gift my Father promised, which you have heard me speak about." What was that gift? Verse 5 tells us: "For John baptized with water, but in a few days you will be baptized with the Holy Spirit." This reminds us of John the Baptist's prediction (Matt. 3:11), which we discussed in our chapter on Matthew.

The key verse of the Book of Acts is Acts 1:8: "But you will receive power when the Holy Spirit comes on you; and you will be my witnesses in Jerusalem, and in all Judea and Samaria, and to the ends of the earth."

This verse gives both the power and program of the Church of Jesus Christ. To elaborate:

> The *power* is the Holy Spirit. The *program* is the evangelization of the world. For a person to claim to be filled with the Spirit and yet not to be vitally concerned about world missions is to deny his profession. When the Holy Spirit fills the human heart with His power and presence, He generates the urge to carry out Christ's command. The converse is also true: the Great Commission cannot be fulfilled without the power of the Spirit. (*Beacon Bible Commentary,* 7:262)

This verse also gives the three main divisions of the Book of Acts: (1) Witnessing in Jerusalem (cc. 1—7); (2) Witnessing in All Judea and Samaria (cc. 8—12); (3) Witnessing in the Gentile World (cc. 13—28). The disciples followed the program their Master had outlined for them.

What we have just noted was preliminary to the "day of Pentecost," which is described in the second chapter of Acts. We are told that the 120 in the Upper Room (1:13, 15) were "all together in one place" (2:1). They were obediently waiting for the fulfillment of Jesus' promise in Acts 1:8.

And then it happened! "Suddenly a sound like the blowing of a violent wind came from heaven and filled the whole house where they were sitting. They saw what seemed to be tongues of fire that separated and came to rest on each of them. All of them were filled with the Holy Spirit and began to speak in other tongues as the Spirit enabled them" (vv. 2-4).

In verses 2-4 three significant symbols accompanied the infilling with the Holy Spirit on the Day of Pentecost. The first was the roaring "sound like the blowing of a violent wind." This was a symbol of the *power* Jesus promised in Acts 1:8. The second was "tongues of fire that separated and came to rest on each of them." This was a symbol of the *purity* John the Baptist promised in Matt. 3:11. The third was the speaking "in other tongues." This was a symbol of the *propagation* of the gospel. And the central thing was that all of them "were filled with the Holy Spirit." This was the greatest miracle of Pentecost.

Have you had your personal Pentecost? The songwriter has phrased the question:

> *Have you ever felt the power*
> *Of the Pentecostal fire,*
> *Burning up all carnal nature,*
> *Cleansing out all base desire,*
> *Going thro' and thro' your spirit,*
> *Cleansing all its stain away?*
> *Oh, I'm glad, so glad to tell you*
> *It is for us all today.*

Today some who emphasize the aspect of power tend to minimize, or even eliminate, that of purity. They deny that when we are filled with the Spirit our hearts are cleansed from all sin. But when Peter was explaining at the Jerusalem Council what had happened to the people in the house of Cornelius, he asserted: "God, who knows the heart, showed that he accepted them by giving the Holy Spirit to them, just as he did to us. He made no distinction between us and them, for he purified their hearts by faith" (Acts 15:8-9). That is, when they were filled with the Spirit, their hearts were "purified." Incidentally, in these two verses "them" means Gentiles and "us" means Jews. The former were to be just as much a part of the Christian church as the latter.

The use of the word *tongues* here in relation to the Day of Pentecost merits a bit of consideration. In verses 4 and 11 the Greek word is *glossais*. The singular is *glossa*, which was used first for the physical tongue in our mouth and then for what was spoken by that tongue.

But we also find in verses 6 and 8 the Greek word *dialectos*, which in that day meant "language" (Acts 1:19; 2:6, 8; 21:40; 22:2; 26:14). It is correctly translated that way in the NASB and NIV (and most versions today). (The KJV translates it as "tongue" in verse 8.)

Now it is perfectly clear that in Acts 2:4-11 the Greek words *glossa* and *dialectos* are used interchangeably as referring to the same thing. In the Upper Room the 120 disciples, when filled with the Holy Spirit, spoke in "other tongues" (v. 4). Then we are told: "Now there were staying in Jerusalem God-fearing Jews from every nation under heaven. When they heard this sound, a crowd came together in bewilderment, because each one heard them speaking in his own language" (vv. 5-6). Knowing that the speakers were *ignorant* "Galileans," the hearers asked each other: "Then how is it that each of us hears them in his own native language?" (v. 8).

There follows in verses 9-11 a list of not less than *15* language areas represented in the crowd that heard the Spirit-filled disciples speaking. In amazement the people were exclaiming, "We hear them declaring the wonders of God in our own tongues!"

No one can deny the obvious fact that the speaking "in other tongues" on the Day of Pentecost was not the use of some unknown tongues but rather the speaking clearly and intelligibly in the known languages of that time, proclaiming the gospel to those who had not heard it. And what was the result of this? Three thousand people were saved that day (v. 41).

Incidentally, some have claimed that with the crowd it was a miracle of *hearing* and not of speaking. But that idea is clearly ruled out by verse 6, where it is stated that "each one heard them speaking in his own language."

A pertinent illustration comes from a Friends district superintendent who once shared an outstanding experience in his spiritual life as a pastor.

He received a call one day to go to the hospital and share the good news of salvation with a man the doctor said would not live through the night. He sat at the bedside of this stranger and tried to converse with him. But he discovered right away that the man did not understand him at all, and neither could the pastor get what the sick man tried to say to him. They did not speak the same language.

Frustrated the pastor prayed earnestly that the Lord would enable him to explain to this dying man how he could be saved. He soon found himself conversing with the patient, who gave his heart to God. But the pastor had no idea what language they were conversing in.

My friend told me: "Sometime later I heard a Norwegian speaking, and the language sounded familiar. I checked with the hospital and found that the patient I had led to the Lord was indeed a Norwegian." That makes sense!

2. The Samaritan Revival (8:5, 14-17)

After Stephen's death by stoning because of his Christian faith (7:54-60), "a great persecution broke out against the church at Jerusalem" (8:1). Then: "Philip went down to a city in Samaria and proclaimed the Christ there" (v. 5). He performed miracles of healing (vv. 6-7), and "there was great joy in that city" (v. 8).

After some space of time there was a second phase in this Samaritan revival, as indicated in verses 14-17: "When the apostles in Jerusalem heard that Samaria had accepted the word of God, they sent Peter and John to them. When they arrived, they prayed for them that they might receive the Holy Spirit, because the Holy Spirit had not yet come upon any of them; they had simply been baptized into the name of the Lord Jesus. Then Peter and John placed their hands on them, and they received the Holy Spirit." These people in Samaria were converted to Christ through the preaching of Philip. Then at a later time they were filled with the Holy Spirit under the ministry of Peter and John. For them there were clearly two distinct spiritual experiences.

This passage does not *prove* that being filled with the Holy Spirit is definitely a second crisis in Christian experience, but it certainly fits in with this pattern. We shall find later, especially in 1 Thessalonians, clear evidence for the "two works of grace," regeneration and sanctification.

3

ROMANS

1. Outline

The Epistle to the Romans is rightly considered to be the most theological of Paul's 13 Epistles. It deals primarily with soteriology—that is, the doctrine of salvation (from *soter,* the Greek word for Savior).

The first eight chapters of the book comprise the doctrinal section. Here we find Paul discussing three doctrines: (1) Sin (1:18—3:20); (2) Justification (3:21—5:21); (3) Sanctification (cc. 6—8). It is interesting to discover that even non-Wesleyan commentators agree that chapters 6—8 deal with the subject of sanctification. So this is the section of the Epistle on which we shall concentrate our attention.

2. Sanctification Through Death to Self (c. 6)

The death of Christ on the Cross was not only to atone for our sins but also to give us deliverance from the inward nature of sin—what has popularly been called "the carnal nature." In verse 6 Paul writes: "For we know that our old self was crucified with him so that the body of sin might be done away with, that we should no longer be slaves to sin." (Incidentally, if you have the first edition of the NIV, change "rendered powerless" to "done away with"—the official wording now.)

Paul goes on to say in verse 7: "Because anyone who has died has been freed from sin." There is widespread teaching today that we can only be "freed from sin"—that is, from the sinful nature (cleansed from all sin)—"in the hour and article of death." But Paul is teaching here, as the context (v. 6) clearly shows, that when by faith we have identified ourselves with Christ on the Cross ("our old self was crucified with him"), then "the body of sin" is "destroyed" (KJV), or "done away with" (NASB, NIV). Then we have died to sin and are "freed from sin"—what theologians call inbred sin or inherited depravity. Paul declares that we can be freed from sin in this life, not just at physical death.

In verse 10 the apostle writes of Christ: "The death he died, he died to sin once for all; but the life he lives, he lives to God." Then he adds the application to us: "In the same way, count yourselves dead to sin but alive to God in Christ Jesus" (v. 11). Obviously, we are not "dead to sin" until the sinful nature—"our old self" (v. 6) has been destroyed by being crucified with Christ. That happens when we by faith "count" ourselves "dead to sin" (v. 11).

3. The Need for Sanctification (c. 7)

In this chapter Paul first deals with life under the Mosaic law (vv. 1-16). In verse 17 he declares that when he did wrong, "It is no longer I myself who do it, but it is sin living in me." He defines this in verse 18 as "my sinful nature." In verse 20 he again calls it "sin living in me." In verses 23 and 25 he designates it "the law of sin."

Is there no hope of deliverance from this inner nature of sin? There is! In verse 24 Paul cries out: "What a wretched man I am! Who will rescue me from this body of death?" In verse 25 we have his cry of victory: "Thanks be to God— through Jesus Christ our Lord!" He can, and will, deliver us

23

from this "sinful nature" (v. 5) as we by faith identify ourselves with Him in His crucifixion, and so die to self. This is the negative side of sanctification.

4. Sanctification Through the Spirit (c. 8)

As noted previously, chapters 6 and 7 present the negative side of sanctification—through being crucified with Christ (6:6) and so becoming "dead to sin" (v. 11)—and thus being rescued from "this body of death" (7:24). Chapter 8 presents the positive side of sanctification: being filled with the Spirit.

The Holy Spirit is not mentioned in chapter 7. In striking contrast, He is named abut 20 times in chapter 8. Here we have life in the Spirit. Paul declares that "through Christ Jesus the law of the Spirit of life set me free from the law of sin and death" (v. 2). Now he could say that he did "not live according to the sinful nature but according to the Spirit" (v. 4). He warns us: "Those controlled by the sinful nature cannot please God" (v. 8).

One of the ministries of the Holy Spirit to us is that He guides and helps us in our prayer life. In verses 26 and 27 Paul writes: "In the same way, the Spirit helps us in our weakness. We do not know what we ought to pray for, but the Spirit himself intercedes for us with groans that words cannot express. And he who searches our hearts knows the mind of the Spirit, because the Spirit intercedes for the saints in accordance with God's will."

4

1 CORINTHIANS

1. Spiritual Gifts (c. 12)

Problem church? Paul had one! That is vividly shown in his First Epistle to the Corinthians. In it he deals with no less than nine problems existing in the Corinthian church. He handles these in a very straightforward, and sometimes stern, fashion.

General Superintendent R. T. Williams once said that the only way to avoid having any problems in a church was this: "Don't take in any new members and chloroform the ones you already have. Every person is a potential problem."

The main problem in the church at Corinth was that of divisions in the congregation. So Paul here says: "There are different kinds of gifts, but the same Spirit. There are different kinds of service, but the same Lord. There are different kinds of working, but the same God works all of them in all men" (vv. 4-6). The unity of the Trinity is to be reflected strongly in the unity of the Church.

Paul then proceeds, in verses 7-11, to name no less than nine gifts of the Spirit. The list ends with "different kinds of tongues" and "interpretation of tongues" (v. 10).

Another list is found in verses 27-30. Again we find "different kinds of tongues" at the very end (v. 28). The fact that this gift is at the bottom of both lists is certainly very significant. "Speaking in different kinds of tongues" was the least gift, not the most important one. And as we saw in our study of the second chapter of Acts, this could very well mean "different languages." One thing is certain: Paul did not treat the gift of tongues as an evidence that one had been filled with the Spirit. It was just one of many gifts of the Spirit, and apparently the least important.

At the very end of this chapter he makes this significant announcement: "And now I will show you the most excellent way." What was that? It was the way of love, as presented beautifully in chapter 13—the great "love chapter" in the Bible. And that chapter begins with these very significant words: "If I speak in the tongues of men and of angels, but have not love, I am only a resounding gong or a clanging cymbal."

Paul continues by saying: "If I have the gift of prophecy and can fathom all mysteries and all knowledge, and if I have a faith that can move mountains, but have not love, I am nothing. If I give all I possess to the poor, and surrender my body to the flames, but have not love, I gain nothing" (vv. 2-3).

Paul's prescription for a problem church is in these three verses. It is not eloquence, knowledge, faith, or good works—four things in which the Corinthians gloried. No; the correct prescription is *love.* That alone will solve their problems. Teresa of Avila (1515-82) said: "Our Lord does not care so much for the importance of our works as for the love with which they are done."

2. Speaking in Tongues (c. 14)

Tying into the whole emphasis of chapter 13, Paul begins chapter 14 by saying: "Follow the way of love and eagerly desire spiritual gifts, especially the gift of prophecy"—or, "preaching." In verses 2-4 the apostle points out the vast superiority of preaching over tongues-speaking. In verse 9 he warns his readers: "Unless you speak intelligible words with your tongue, how will anyone know what you are saying? You will just be speaking into the air." In verse 12 he exhorts his readers: "Since you are eager to have spiritual gifts, try to excel in gifts that build up the church."

Six times in this chapter the KJV has the expression "*unknown* tongue" (vv. 2, 4, 13, 14, 19, 27). Today *italics* are used for added emphasis. In the KJV italics are used for words that are not in the inspired Greek text. There is apparently no justification for adding "unknown."

Verse 18 is a favorite with those who emphasize speaking in tongues. Paul writes: "I thank God that I speak in tongues more than all of you." What did he mean?

Adam Clarke, the leading early Wesleyan commentator, gives this good answer:

> He understood more languages than any of them did; and this was indispensably necessary, as he was the apostle of the Gentiles in general, and had to preach to different provinces where different dialects, if not languages, were used. . . . it is very probable that he knew more languages than any man in the church of Corinth. (*Commentary on the Holy Bible*, 1-vol. ed., 1118)

This fits in perfectly with what we found in our study of the second chapter of Acts, that the speaking in tongues on the Day of Pentecost was unquestionably a speaking in the known, intelligible languages of that day. This was necessary for the effective proclamation of the gospel at that event, where the crowd included people from 15 different language areas. That, however, would not be true in the congregation at Corinth. And so Paul says: "But in the church I would rather speak five intelligible words to instruct others than ten thousand words in a tongue" (v. 19). The situation at Corinth was so bad that Paul adds this gentle(?) reproof: "Brothers, stop thinking like children. In regard to evil be infants, but in your thinking be adults" (v. 20). Good advice!

To be fair, we should perhaps acknowledge that some good commentators hold that the speaking in tongues at Corinth was a matter of ecstatic utterance. We would not rule that out. There are some matters, even of biblical interpretation, for which we will not have the final, full answers until we get to heaven.

* * *

The first four chapters of this book have looked into Matthew, Acts, Romans, and 1 Corinthians. The next five chapters will be in the form of sermons on outstanding passages on sanctification in Galatians, Ephesians, 1 Thessalonians, Hebrews, and 1 Peter. We hope that these sermons will preach themselves into the hearts and minds of many of our readers for their spiritual good. God grant that it may be so.

5

GALATIANS
Let Me Die!

Scripture: Gal. 2:20; 3:1-3; 5:16-25
Text: Gal. 2:20

Introduction:

Every resurrection must be preceded by a crucifixion. You can't come to Easter Sunday without going through Good Friday. That's a chronological fact, but it has theological implications. You can't reach the empty tomb unless you take the road that goes through the Garden of Gethsemane and past the Cross of Calvary. One of the great paradoxes of Christianity is simply this: You have to die to live!

I. The Crucifixion of the Carnal Self

George Mueller, that great man of faith of Bristol, England, once said: "There was a day when I died, utterly died." And on his 90th birthday he wrote these words:

I was converted in November, 1825, but I only came into the full surrender of the heart four years later, in July, 1829. The love of money was gone, the love of place was gone, the love of position was gone, the love of worldly pleasures was gone. God, God alone became my portion.

He also wrote: "After I was filled with the Spirit, I learned more about the Scriptures in four hours than I had learned in the previous four years."

It should be noted that George Mueller used two expressions to describe the experience that came to him four years after his conversion. First, he called it "the full surrender of the heart." That's our part. We have to surrender our will fully to God's will. In the second place, he called it being "filled with the Spirit." That's God's part. God made us with free wills; so He can't compel us to surrender our wills to His will. We have to do it voluntarily. On the other hand, we can't fill ourselves with the Holy Spirit. *God* has to do that. But when we *do* surrender our wills fully to Him, He *will* fill us with His Spirit.

One of the great British New Testament scholars of our generation was Vincent Taylor. He declared: "Sin is self-coronation." Alongside that is what I believe to be a corollary truth: "Sanctification is self-crucifixion." Ultimately we either let self be crucified and Christ crowned as Lord of all, or, refusing to do this, self is crowned as Lord of all in our lives, and Christ is crucified afresh by our self-will.

Jesus said: "Whoever loses his life for me will find it" (Matt. 16:25). We sing: "Let me lose myself and find it Lord, in Thee." The only way we can really *find* ourselves is to *lose* ourselves in Christ.

Nowhere is the application of that truth more significantly stated than in our text for today, Gal. 2:20. The KJV states: "I am crucified with Christ: nevertheless I live; yet not I, but Christ liveth in me."

In the original Greek the first clause of this verse says: *Christo synestauromai*—"with Christ I have been crucified." The pefect tense in Greek emphasizes two things: (1) a completed act; (2) a continuing state. What the Greek says here is: "I have been, and still am, crucified with Christ."

In the KJV the second clause reads: "Nevertheless I live."
But the original Greek says just the opposite: *zo de ouketi
ego*—"and *no longer* do I live." *Ouketi* cannot mean "nevertheless." It means "no longer." And the *ego* (taken over into
English as "ego") is emphatic: "no longer do *I* live."

The Greek text of the third clause reads: *ze de en emoi
christos*—"but in me lives Christ." What Paul is saying is this:
"Christ has taken the place of the carnal ego in control of my
life." That is what it means to be sanctified wholly (1 Thess.
5:23). We experience both a crucifixion with Christ and also a
new resurrection life in Him.

II. The Work of Faith (3:3)

In the Epistle to the Galatians Paul presents sanctification not only as the crucifixion of the carnal self (2:20) but
also as the work of faith (3:3). Starting in the middle of verse
2, Paul poses critical questions: "Did you receive the Spirit by
observing the law, or by believing what you heard? Are you
so foolish? After beginning with the Spirit, are you now trying to attain your goal [or, reach perfection] by human effort?"

A careful reading of this Epistle will show exactly why
Paul wrote it. He and Barnabas, on their first missionary jour-
ney (Acts 13—14), had founded churches in the Roman
province of Galatia, which was in the center of Asia Minor
(modern Turkey). Later Paul heard that some Judaizers had
gone in and told the new Gentile converts that in order to be
saved they had to be circumcised and keep the law of Moses.

Perhaps some of the converts protested: "Paul told us
that all we had to do to be saved was to repent and believe on
the Lord Jesus. We did believe, and we know we *are* saved."

I can almost hear the Judaizers say: "Yes, but if you want
to be made perfect" (3:3, KJV), "you must keep all the outward ordinances of the Mosaic law."

31

Paul protested against this. In essence he told them: "You were justified through faith; you will be sanctified through faith. It is all of faith."

But what does faith mean?

John G. Paton was the pioneer missionary to the New Hebrides. Arriving there, he soon learned the language so that he could preach the gospel to the people.

Then he felt the need of translating the Word of God into their language, so they could read it for themselves. But he ran into a serious problem: Their language was full of *concrete* terms, but almost entirely lacking in *abstract* ones. They had words for "house," "tree," "stone," and so forth, but nothing for "love," "joy," or "peace." Worst of all he found no word suggesting the idea of believing. How can you tell people to believe in the Lord Jesus Christ when they have no word for "believe"?

One day he was sitting in his rude hut, feeling frustrated with his problem. Suddenly the door opened and an old man entered. He had walked a long distance and was tired. So he slumped down in a chair. As he did so, he said, "I'm leaning my whole weight on this chair."

Immediately the Holy Spirit said to John G. Paton, "That's it!" He turned to the man and asked, "What did you say?"

"I'm leaning my whole weight on this chair."

In the New Testament for that primitive tribe, "Believe on Jesus" became: "Lean your whole weight on Jesus." That's what faith really is!

III. The Fruit of the Spirit (5:22-23)

In the Epistle to the Galatians sanctification is presented not only as the crucifixion of the carnal self (2:20) and the work of faith (3:3) but also as the fruit of the Spirit (5:22-23).

The word *but* at the beginning of verse 22 should be heavily underscored: It points up the colossal contrast be-

32

tween "the works of the flesh" and "the fruit of the Spirit." Every one of the works of the flesh listed in verses 19-21 is divisive: divisive of nations, of communities, of churches, of homes, and worst of all, of hearts.

In contrast to this, every characteristic mentioned in verses 22 and 23 is a uniting element. And the greatest uniting force in all the world is love. "The fruit of the Spirit is love."

People often speak of "the fruits of the Spirit." But that is unscriptural. The Bible does not use that expression anywhere. It says, "the fruit of the Spirit."

"Yes," you say, "but these verses proceed to list nine items. How can you use the singular verb here?"

John Wesley made a helpful suggestion at this point in his *Explanatory Notes upon the New Testament,* published in 1755. He said of "love": "It is the root of all the rest."

This is logically sound. The Bible says, "God is love" (1 John 4:8, 16). It also clearly teaches that the Holy Spirit is God. So when our hearts are filled with the Holy Spirit, they are filled with love. Then this agape love will show itself in joy, peace, patience, and the other things mentioned here.

Entire sanctification means "perfect love" (1 John 4:16-18). That was John Wesley's favorite designation for this experience.

The first thing that love produces is "joy." What is joy?

Once when I was holding an evangelistic campaign in a church, I noticed a girl in the audience who never smiled. It was depressing! I couldn't get a smile out of her, no matter how hard I tried.

Years later I returned to that church. Sue was smiling all over! Eagerly I asked somebody what had happened to Sue since I was there previously. The person replied: "Oh, didn't you know? She has fallen in love with John."

If falling in love with another human being can make a person come alive like that, what ought falling in love with Jesus do to us? It should fill us with joy!

Someone has said: "Joy is the echo of God's life within us." Also: "Joy is the reflection of spiritual health in the soul." This is scriptural. We are all familiar with the Old Testament declaration: "The joy of the Lord is your strength" (Neh. 8:10). A joyful Christian is a strong Christian! And let us not forget: A joyless Christian is a weak Christian. Let's rejoice in the Lord and be strong!

The next item is "peace." The Greek word is *eirene,* from which we get "Irene." Any girl with that name should be a peaceful person!

When we are justified freely, we have peace *with* God through our Lord Jesus Christ. When we are sanctified wholly, the peace *of* God fills our souls, because the civil war inside between the old carnal nature with which we were born and the new Christ nature that came in at conversion has been ended by the full surrender of our will to God's will and the consequent crucifixion of the carnal self—as we have already noted.

Dr. J. B. Chapman once said: "Peace is the consciousness of adequate resources to meet every emergency of life."

In the depression days, my wife and I once invited another couple to eat lunch with us in a restaurant. As we were waiting for the waitress to come, I suddenly felt uneasy. Under the tablecloth I pulled out my wallet. My worst fears were confirmed: I only had a five dollar bill! Desperately I prayed: "Lord, help them to order a small hamburg sandwich!"

One day I took care of that forever: I got an American Express Card. Now I can say to guests, "Order whatever you like." That little green card will take care of even lobster tail! When we are filled with the Holy Spirit we have that peace because we know that *He* can handle any emergency that may confront us!

34

The next item is "patience." The Greek word is *macrothymia*, which is correctly translated "longsuffering" in the KJV.

All human beings have different personality traits: we differ in our likes and dislikes, in our tastes and preferences. So we have to be longsuffering with each other, even as sanctified Christians. But if the Holy Spirit fills our hearts with divine love, He can help us learn to practice patience with each other.

The next virtue is "kindness." In 1 Cor. 13:4 Paul also puts these two together in the same order: "Love is patient, love is kind." Instinctively we feel that kindness is one of the main manifestations of love. Let's practice it, then! Our lives should show kindness to everybody every day.

We should remember, however, that it takes time for fruit to grow. If I plant an apple tree, I don't go out the next day to pick ripe apples off it. So we should allow time for the newly sanctified to show the fruit of the Spirit growing in their lives. And we should not allow Satan to browbeat us if we are not showing the full fruit of kindness right away.

The next thing that love produces is "goodness." What is goodness?

Some people think that because they don't lie, cheat, steal, or do any "bad things" they are good. But goodness is not a negative thing; it is positive.

The best definition of goodness I have read is in Charles R. Erdman's commentary on Galatians. He says that goodness is "love in action." We are not good because of anything we don't do; we are only good as we are acting in love. That truth confronts all of us with a tremendous challenge!

The next virtue is "faithfulness." The Greek word *pistis* means both "faith" and "faithfulness." But the context clearly shows that here the latter is meant, as all new versions have.

Paul goes on to say that love shows itself in "gentleness." The main symbol of the Holy Spirit in the Bible is the gentle dove. That is shown by the fact that in all three Synoptic Gospels we are told that at Jesus' baptism the Holy Spirit came down on Him as a dove (Matt. 3:16; Mark 1:10; Luke 3:22).

In the Song of Songs we find doves mentioned many times. In one passage (1:15), the Lover says to his Beloved:

> "How beautiful you are, my darling!
> Oh, how beautiful!
> Your eyes are doves."

Unfortunately, some professing Christians do not have eyes like a dove; they have hawk's eyes!

We have seen a hawk soaring very high in the sky. Suddenly it took a power dive, grabbed a chicken or field mouse in its beak, and flew off to devour it. We wondered how the hawk could spot that tiny object so far away, and we were told that hawk's eyes have telescopic lens.

If we are proud that we can spot the least little fault in others, let's ask God to take off those telescopic lens and install wide-angle lens, so we can see life and see it whole. Perhaps if we had the background of that person we criticize, we would be worse than he is!

The last virtue mentioned is "self-control." This is more than "temperance" (KJV). It is a matter of keeping our whole life—our actions, words, and attitudes—under control by the help of the Spirit.

Conclusion:

Rees Howells was converted in the United States about the time of the great Welsh Revival. Returning to Wales, he soon started out preaching the gospel in villages around him, and God gave him souls.

But one day the Holy Spirit began to deal with him definitely about a deeper need of his heart. He describes it this way:

It was unconditional surrender. . . . It took five days to make the decision. Like Isaiah, I saw the holiness of God, and seeing Him, I saw my own corrupt nature. . . . I knew I had to be cleansed.

He continues: "First there was the love of money." Finally came the fifth day of his dying out to himself. The Holy Spirit asked him: "Now, are you willing?"

Rees Howells wanted to say yes, but he found himself unable to do so. Again the Spirit spoke: "I have been dealing with you for five days; you must give me your decision by six o'clock tonight."

Rees Howells writes: "I asked Him for more time, but He said, 'You will not have a minute after six o'clock.'"

Once more the Spirit asked, "Are you willing?"

Rees Howells tells us: "It was ten minutes to six. . . . Five to six came. I could count the ticks of the clock."

Finally came the climax. He records:

Then the Spirit spoke again: "If you can't be willing, would you like me to help you? Are you willing to be made willing?". . . . It was one minute to six. I bowed my head and said, "Lord, I am willing." . . . Within an hour the Third Person of the Godhead had come in. (*Rees Howells, Intercessor,* 43)

What is the price we pay to receive this experience? We have to die out to self, surrender our will fully to God's will.

The songwriter put it well:

> *All to Jesus I surrender.*
> *Make me, Saviour, wholly thine;*
> *Let me feel the Holy Spirit,*
> *Truly know that Thou art mine.*

The chorus:

> *I surrender all. I surrender all.*
> *All to Thee, my blessed Saviour, I surrender all.*

Will you make that your prayer? Right now?

6

EPHESIANS
The Holy Church

Scripture: Eph. 1:3, 13-14; 4:30; 5:25-33
Text: Eph. 5:25-27

Introduction:

We are faced with a real challenge in three outstanding expressions in the first chapter of Ephesians.

The first one is in the third verse. In the KJV it is translated "in heavenly places," in the NIV "in the heavenly realms." The Greek has simply: *en tois epouraniois*—literally, "in the heavenlies." It occurs five times in this Epistle and is really the keynote of Ephesians, which presents life in the heavenlies. It is in *heavenly fellowship* with Christ that we experience "every spiritual blessing" (singular in the Greek), as verse 3 tells us, "Fellowship divine! Oh, what blessed, sweet communion!"

The second expression is in verse 13. It is the verb *sealed* (KJV). When we speak now of "sealing" a letter we mean licking the glue and fastening the flap on the envelope. The Greek verb *sphragizo* means to "stamp with a seal." The NIV says: "you were marked in him [Christ] with a seal."

Archaeologists have dug up many cylindrical seals from the Babylonian and Persian periods. A servant would take a piece of soft clay and mold it into a cylinder about the size of the human thumb. On this round clay cylinder he would inscribe the insignia of his master. Then he would bake it hard in a kiln.

When the master wanted to send a bale of goods down the Euphrates River, the servant would put soft wax where the bundle was tied together. Then on this soft wax he would make a complete rotation of the cylindrical seal, leaving an oblong imprint of the master's insignia. This would show that the bundle belonged to this particular man.

In the period when Paul wrote, the seal was a signet ring worn by every wealthy Roman. He would stamp the wax with his ring.

The point is this: No man had a right to place his seal on anything unless it was really his property. Just so, God cannot stamp us with His seal, the Holy Spirit, until we give ourselves wholly to Him. When we surrender our will completely to His will, to be His—body, soul, and spirit, for time and eternity—then God will mark us in Christ with a seal, the promised Holy Spirit.

Our third expression is in verse 14. The Greek word is *arrabon* (KJV, "earnest").

The earliest meaning of this, found in classical Greek, is "a down payment guaranteeing that the rest will be paid." So we read that the Holy Spirit is "a deposit guaranteeing our inheritance" (NIV). The Holy Spirit is the down payment on our heavenly home. What will heaven be like? It will be like those times when the Holy Spirit makes the presence of Jesus most real to our hearts. That is a foretaste of heaven.

The word *arrabon* (in the form *arrabona*) has a very striking use in modern Greek, where it means "an engagement ring." This is a very beautiful thought. When we are converted, there begins a loving courtship with Christ. But finally He asks, "Will you be Mine, only Mine, forever Mine?" If we say a full yes to that, He slips the engagement ring on our finger, the Holy Spirit in our heart.

It is important that we keep this heavenly engagement ring. Eph. 4:30 urges: "And do not grieve the Holy Spirit of God, with whom you were sealed for the day of redemption."

How may we grieve the Holy Spirit? Certainly by deliberate disobedience. But we can also grieve Him by ignoring Him, making Him the unwelcome guest in our hearts. Unwelcome guests usually leave!

Now to consider our text—Eph. 5:25-27. Verse 25 points out *the provision for our sanctification in the death of Christ,* in verse 26 *the prerequisite of our sanctification in the washing of regeneration,* and in verse 27 *the purpose of our sanctification in our presentation to Christ as His bride.*

I. The Provision for Our Sanctification in the Death of Christ

The Golden Text of the Bible is John 3:16: "For God so loved the world that he gave his one and only Son, that whoever believes in him shall not perish but have eternal life." Now, in Eph. 5:25-26 we find: "Husbands, love your wives, just as Christ loved the church and gave himself up for her to make her holy."

Heb. 13:12 corroborates this. It says: "And so Jesus also suffered outside the city gate to make the people holy [or, sanctify the people] through his own blood." When we realize that Christ suffered on the Cross not only to save us but also to sanctify us, it should warn us of the terrible ingratitude we show when we do not go on and get sanctified wholly. We should not let His sufferings for our sanctification be in vain!

II. The Prerequisite of Our Sanctification in the Washing of Regeneration

We go on now to verse 26: That he might *"make her holy* [sanctify her], cleansing her by the washing with water through the word" (NIV) or, "the washing of regeneration" (Titus 3:5, KJV).

"Cleansing" here is the aorist participle *catherisas*. Greek grammars agree that the aorist participle normally indicates action antecedent to the main verb. So the correct translation is: "having cleansed." What the Greek says is that Christ, having cleansed the church in the washing of regeneration, purposes to sanctify her. And "sanctify" here is in the aorist subjunctive, suggesting a crisis experience rather than a long, drawn-out process.

Incidentally, the Greek word for "church," *ecclesia* (v. 25), is feminine, and all the pronouns that refer back to it are feminine in Greek. Furthermore, the picture here is of the church as the bride of Christ (see vv. 31-32). And since a bride is not an "it" (KJV), the word is "her" (NIV).

And now to the third point, in verse 27:

III. The Purpose of Our Sanctification in Our Presentation to Christ as His Bride

Why did Christ die on the Cross? In order that having cleansed His Church with the washing of regeneration, and sanctified her, He might "present her to himself as a radiant church, without stain or wrinkle or any other blemish, but holy and blameless."

The expression "without stain or wrinkle" suggests to us the idea of being "washed and ironed." Let's pursue that idea.

I have watched my wife turn on the hot water in the washing machine and put detergent in it. Then she puts in some soiled clothes. I can almost hear them groaning as they are shoved down in that hot, sudsy water. Then she pushes a button and the agitator pushes those clothes around. By now I can almost hear them groaning out loud.

Then comes the second stage. Before we had electric dryers, there was a wringer on the top of the washing machine. I liked to tuck a corner of the mouth of a pillow slip in between the rollers. As the rollers kept turning, the mouth of that pillow slip would finally be closed. Some people I knew never did go through God's wringer because they never got their big mouths shut!

Still the rollers would turn relentlessly. The pillow slip would fight back, puffing up more and more. But finally it would come out flat. And I know again that some people have never gone through God's wringer because they never got their puff and pride squeezed out of them.

But one stage was still left—the ironing board. For Jesus wants His bride to be "without stain or wrinkle." And when we meet Him as our heavenly Bridegroom at the "wedding supper of the Lamb" (Rev. 19:9), we want to be sure that we are "without stain or wrinkle" as we are presented to Him. So let's get the wrinkles out of our personalities by submitting to the Holy Spirit's ironing process. It doesn't feel comfortable, but it's important. And that ironing process goes on throughout our lives down here.

Many years ago I heard a man give a striking testimony at a camp meeting. He had been a civil engineer commissioned by our government to plot the path of the Pan American highway through Central America.

After many days of hard work in the hot sun, he received a telegram from Washington asking him to come back immediately. So he hastened down to the harbor city to catch a plane back to the States. He went to sleep, dreaming of a nice cool flight back home.

But that night God called him on the heavenly phone. "Where are you going tomorrow?"

"I'm going back to Washington."

Then the Lord said, "I have another errand for you to take care of first. You remember that new convert Pedro up in the mountains? He is walking in all the light he has, but his heart is hungry for a deeper experience. I want you to go back and tell him how to be sanctified wholly."

"But Lord, my boss told me to come back to Washington immediately."

The Lord answered him, "Who is your boss, anyway?"

This man was sanctified wholly, and so he promptly replied, "You are, Lord. But I was told that they had some great project waiting for me, like plotting another Panama or Suez Canal."

I shall never forget what the man next related in his testimony. Looking very serious, he told us: "The Lord said to me, 'I'm a lot more interested in Pedro being sanctified wholly than I am in your becoming a great, world-renowned engineer.'"

We need to get God's perspective on life. He puts the highest premium on our having a clean heart and living a holy life. Have *you* been sanctified wholly? If not, make this your prayer:

> *Lord Jesus, I long to be perfectly whole;*
> *I want Thee forever to live in my soul.*
> *Break down every idol, cast out every foe.*
> *Now wash me and I shall be whiter than snow.*

"Whiter than snow" means that we have been inwardly cleansed from the sinful nature. We are clean through and through.

7

1 THESSALONIANS
Sanctification: The Will of God

Scripture: 1 Thess. 1:4-10; 3:12—4:7; 5:23-24
Text: 1 Thess. 4:3—"It is God's will that you should be
sanctified."

Introduction:

Two important questions are often asked of us who are
of the Wesleyan persuasion. The first is: "Where do you get
the term *entire sanctification?*"

The answer is found clearly in 1 Thess. 5:23. The KJV
states it: "And the very God of peace sanctify you wholly."
This means entire sanctification. In fact, the *New American
Standard Bible* has "sanctify you entirely."

The Greek adverb is *holoteleis,* found only here in the
New Testament. It is a strong compound, composed of *holos*
—"whole, complete, entire"—and *telos,* "end." So it literally
means "wholly-completely" or "completely-entirely."

In his famous German New Testament, made in 1522,
Martin Luther translated this compound as *durch und durch,*
"through and through." I suggested to our Committee on Bible Translation that we adopt this English rendering for the

NIV, and it was done. Later I discovered that the Arndt and Gingrich *Greek-English Lexicon of the New Testament* suggested "through and through" for this passage. So the New Testament does teach entire sanctification as a complete cleansing from all sin.

The second question is: "Why do you say that this is a second crisis in Christian experience, after conversion?"

To find the answer to this question we must turn back to the first chapter. There in verse 9 Paul is addressing those who "turned to God from idols to serve the living and true God." In other words, the readers of this Epistle were born-again Christians who had forsaken their pagan background to serve the Lord.

Also in verse 7 Paul writes: "And so you became a model to all the believers in Macedonia and Achaia." These new converts were living exemplary Christian lives. They were not backslidden; they were even *model* Christians.

In the third place, the apostle says in verse 8: "The Lord's message rang out from you not only in Macedonia and Achaia—your faith in God has become known everywhere." Here were people who were genuinely converted, living exemplary lives, and propagating the good news of salvation. And yet Paul wrote to them: "It is God's will that *you* should be sanctified" (4:3). Entire sanctification is not something for sinners, but only for believers. It is definitely a "second work of grace."

There are three things to consider in connection with the meaning of entire sanctification. It means: (1) Purity; (2) Power; and (3) Perfect Love.

I. Purity

Under the general heading of "purity" first think of "purity of life."

There once was a party of tourists visiting a coal mine. Before they descended to the tunnel below, the old guide who was assigned to them brought out some coveralls and suggested they put them on to protect their clothes from the coal dust in the mine.

In the group was a girl who was wearing a pretty white dress. (This must have been a long time ago!) She didn't want to put on those ugly coveralls, and so protested. When the guide rather insisted, she got a bit uppish and said, "I guess I can go down into that coal mine with this white dress on, if I want to."

The old man looked at her a moment in silence and then gently replied: "Yes, you can go down into the mine with that white dress, but you can't come back out of the coal mine with a white dress on."

I have had many young people say to me, "Can't I be a Christian and go here or there, or do this or that?" That is a completely wrong question to ask. What we should be asking is: "Can I do this or that, go to this place or the other, and come back as good a Christian as I was before?" That is the *real* question.

I also heard of a man who, one morning, was dressing to go to his office. Meanwhile, his wife was dutifully getting breakfast in the kitchen.

Suddenly he called from the bedroom: "Martha, Martha, come here quick and tell me whether this shirt's clean enough to wear another day."

Wisely, Martha didn't leave the porridge to burn over on the stove. Instead she called back: "No, Henry, there's no need for me to come in and look at that shirt. If it's doubtful, it's dirty." And I submit to you that if a man thought it was doubtful, it surely was dirty!

From this incident I have deduced this important motto: "If in doubt, *don't!*" There are plenty of undoubtedly good things to take up all our time and attention every day without our fooling around with anything that is at all doubtful.

In 1 Thess. 4:7 Paul writes: "For God did not call us to be impure, but to live a holy life." A holy life is a clean life, a godly life. In this day of careless, and even promiscuous, living, we must be careful to live according to God's standards, as set out in His Word.

Sanctification means not only purity of life but also purity of heart. Let us look again at 1 Thess. 5:23. God wants to sanctify us "through and through," cleansing our hearts from all sin and filling them with His Holy Spirit. Furthermore, the verb *sanctify* here is in the aorist tense, which suggests a momentary act. We are to have a crisis experience of complete cleansing.

Cleansing from what? Many of us have heard most of our lives that we are to be cleansed from the carnal nature. But what is carnality?

I once heard a preacher say that he saw a woman get a little tense one day. She excused herself by saying, "It's my nerves." The preacher exclaimed: "Nerves—nonsense! It's sheer carnality!"

I'd like to tie that preacher into a kitchen for a few hours. He's trying to cook something on the stove. A little two-year-old daughter is tugging at his clothes and whining that she doesn't feel good. About that time the baby wakes up in the bedroom and begins to scream his head off. He starts for the bedroom, only to be interrupted by the front doorbell ringing. As he heads for that, the telephone buzzes loudly. I'd like to see then if he had any nerves!

The truth is that nerves are a part of our physical body. We all have them. But we *do* need to learn to control them by the help of the indwelling Holy Spirit. That is a part of growth in grace, after we are sanctified.

In our first pastorate we had an evangelist who asserted emphatically from the pulpit: "All impatience is carnality!" Where do we draw the line between patience and impatience? All of us are relatively patient and yet sometimes feel a bit impatient to get moving. No; impatience, in and of itself, is not carnality.

"Oh," you say, "I know what carnality is; it's anger." Well, if that be true, then Jesus was carnal. In Mark 3:5 we read that Jesus "looked around at them in anger," being "deeply distressed at their stubborn hearts." The Pharisees didn't want Jesus to heal the man with the withered hand because it was the Sabbath day; let the man suffer another 24 hours.

The verb *looked around* is *periblepsamenos,* an aorist participle including a momentary flash of anger at the cruel, selfish attitude of these religious leaders. But "deeply distressed"—or "being grieved" (KJV)—is the present tense of continuous attitude. We are immediately to abhor sin but always to love the sinner.

What, then, is carnality, or "the sinful nature" as we call it in the NIV? It is self-will, wishing to have our own way rather than God's way. That is what God wants to cleanse from our hearts in the experience of entire sanctification.

We need not only purity of life and purity of heart but also purity of mind. In entire sanctification "the body of sin" (Rom. 6:6) is "destroyed" (KJV) or "done away with" (NIV). But though this happens to the sinful nature, our human nature still remains. Holiness does not dehumanize us.

Some people say, "It doesn't matter what I look at or listen to; my heart is pure." I don't buy that! I don't believe that young people can sit and look at everything on television for hours at a time without its affecting their spiritual experience. We can't fill our mind with filth without some of it filtering down into our heart. Let's be careful what we look at, and guard our thoughts carefully.

II. Power

Sanctification is not only purity but power. The word *power* occurs only once in 1 Thessalonians, in 1:5. Paul writes: "Our gospel came to you not simply with words, but also with power, with the Holy Spirit"—that is, with the power of the Holy Spirit. Jesus said to His disciples: "You will receive power when the Holy Spirit comes on you" (Acts 1:8).

The Greek word for "power" is *dynamis,* from which we get three English words: *dynamite, dynamo,* and *dynamic.* These suggest that the Holy Spirit gives us explosive power to overcome all obstacles, electric power being generated in our hearts and lives every day, and excelling power to live dynamic lives and to make us soul winners.

Some time ago I read of a wealthy American who bought a Rolls Royce. He was delighted with its seemingly unlimited power. But, like most men, he wanted to know how many horsepower it had.

The dealer said, "I don't know." When the owner insisted that he find out, the dealer wrote to the company in England. Finally he called the owner and told him that he had received a reply. "How many horsepower?" asked the man. The dealer answered: "I received a telegram of just one word: 'Adequate.'" That is what the Holy Spirit gives us: adequate power to meet every emergency in life!

III. Perfect Love

The third thing that sanctification means is perfect love, as described clearly in 1 John 4:16-18. Here in 1 Thess. 3:12-13 we read about this love that fills our hearts and overflows to others.

The Greek language has three words for love. The lowest term is *eros,* which we have taken over into English in the adjective *erotic.* As this suggests, the word *eros* had bad connotations. It is never used in the New Testament. I call it "Hollywood love."

The second word is *philia.* It occurs only once in the New Testament, in James 4:4 where it is translated "friendship." The related verb *phileo* is translated "kiss" as well as "love."

So *philia* is friendship love, affectionate love. I call it "homey love."

But the dominant word for love in the New Testament is *agape*, which means unselfish love that seeks the highest good of its object. That is the word here. It means "holy love." Paul prayed that the love of the Thessalonian Christians might overflow. Only that which is full can overflow.

Dr. Nathan Wood was president of Gordon Divinity School. Both Mrs. Earle and I took a course in theology under him. We agreed that if we ever saw a person who was filled with the Holy Spirit, Dr. Wood was that.

One day, after teaching morning classes at Eastern Nazarene College, I went into Boston for an afternoon class at Gordon. When I arrived, the place seemed deserted. Puzzled, I looked around and soon discovered the faculty and students gathered in chapel for an all day of prayer.

Quietly entering, I heard one student after another stand up and pray out loud. Two petitions I heard particularly impressed me. A student would pray, "Lord, cleanse my heart from all sin." Then another would pray, "O Lord, fill me with Your Holy Spirit."

When the meeting broke up, I asked Dr. Wood if I could talk with him in his office. I shared my concern about the students' petitions in chapel. When they drew near to the Lord in an all day of prayer, their hearts cried out to be cleansed. But in class I heard professors say that we can't be cleansed from all sin until the time of our physical death. I then mentioned the student's petition to be filled with the Spirit. But we were told in class that we were filled with the Spirit at the time of our conversion. I also remarked that I didn't hear much at Gordon about the Holy Spirit.

To my surprise, instead of arguing with me, Dr. Wood nodded his head in agreement. "I'm afraid our younger professors don't know much about the Holy Spirit," he said. Then he related to me this incident.

He was sitting on the platform during the commencement exercises at his alma mater, Wheaton College, waiting for the honorary D.D. degree to be conferred on him. As the exercises were going on, he felt a cry rising in his heart: "O Lord, I'm not fit to be called a doctor of divinity." Of course, "Divinity" here is to be taken in the objective sense of theology. But it was typical of this man that he thought of it in the subjective sense of divine nature.

Dr. Wood told me that he finally became oblivious to all that was going on around him. Desperately he was crying out in his soul: "O Lord, fix me up inside so I'll be fit to be called a doctor of divinity!"

Just then he heard his name called. He stood to his feet and listened as the citation was read. Then he stepped forward. He told me this: "As the president and the dean draped the doctor's hood down over my head and on to my shoulders, I felt something like an electric shock go through me, from the top of my head to the tip of my toes, and I received a mighty baptism of the Holy Spirit." No wonder we sensed that he was a Spirit-filled man! He was asked to go throughout New England speaking in Baptist churches on the Holy Spirit. He said that people were eager to hear about his experience at Wheaton.

Let us pray this prayer:

> *Have Thine own way, Lord!*
> *Have thine own way!*
> *Hold o'er my being*
> *Absolute sway!*
> *Fill with Thy Spirit*
> *Till all shall see*
> *Christ only, always,*
> *Living in me!*

8

HEBREWS

The Perseverance of the Saints

Scripture: Heb. 12:1-3, 14
Text: Heb. 12:14

Introduction:

Nineteen hundred fifty-four was a great year in the world of athletics. For the first time in recorded history the mile was officially run in less than four minutes. And two men did it that year.

On May 6, Roger Bannister, a 25-year-old English medical student ran a mile in 3 minutes, 59.4 seconds.

On June 21, John Landy, a 24-year-old Australian, ran it in 3 minutes, 58 seconds.

On August 7 these two 4-minute milers competed together, for the first time, in the British games at Vancouver, B.C., in the so-called Miracle Mile. There were many other competitors that day. But instinctively all the spectators knew that either Bannister or Landy would win.

Sure enough, when the pistol cracked, these two men were soon out in front of all the rest. Landy led until the last

100 yards. Then he became obsessed with the question: "Where's Roger?"

Finally, he couldn't stand it any longer, and he looked over his shoulder. And there was Roger, right behind him. But as Landy turned to look, he fumbled a step, and Bannister surged past him to win the race in 3 minutes, 58.8 seconds. Landy came in a poor second at 3 minutes, 59.6 seconds. He lost the race by eight-tenths of a second! What could possibly be more frustrating?

But here's the point. *Time* magazine recorded in 1954 that Landy said to newspaper reporters: "If I hadn't turned to look at Roger, I would have won."

This brings us to our Scripture lesson at the beginning of the 12th chapter of Hebrews, verse 1: "Therefore, since we are surrounded by such a great cloud of witnesses, let us throw off everything that hinders and the sin that so easily entangles, and let us run with perseverance the race marked out for us."

The first word, "Therefore," always points back to what immediately precedes. And what is that here? It is the great "faith chapter" of the Bible: Hebrews 11. There are the names of many of the Old Testament heroes of faith. They are filling the grandstands, as it were, and cheering us on. We can almost hear them shouting: "We made it through to the end, and you can too!"

The author of Hebrews then gives a fourfold exhortation. First he urges us: "Let us throw off everything that hinders."

We never did see anyone winning a race while wearing hip boots and a heavy overcoat—not unless it was a handicap race. From ancient Greek runners in the famous Marathon races, participants have always stripped down to the barest necessities. And we must "throw off" all worldly baggage if we are going to run the Christian race successfully. All hindrances must be discarded immediately.

For the second exhortation, the writer adds: "and the sin that so easily entangles." The KJV says: "and the sin which doth so easily beset us." Thus, people think it means some "besetting sin" they are guilty of. The Greek literally says: "and the sin that clings so closely to us." Twice in the seventh chapter of Romans Paul uses the expression: "sin living in me" (vv. 17, 20). He also calls it: "the law of sin at work within my members" (v. 23). In Rom. 8:7 he refers to it as "the carnal mind" (KJV) or "the sinful mind" (NIV). In many circles it has commonly been called "the carnal nature." It is the greatest single hindrance to our running the Christian race. We need to have our hearts cleansed from "all sin" (1 John 1:7), if we are going to be free to run with full strength. Sin weakens us.

The third exhortation is: "Let us run with perseverance the race marked out for us." The KJV says, "with patience." But it takes more than patience to win a race; it takes *perseverance!* The Greek word literally means "endurance." That is what it takes to win a long-distance race. And the Christian race lasts all the rest of our lives. So we must have "perseverance."

The fourth exhortation is found in verse 2. Now we come to the application of our opening illustration, for it says: "Let us fix our eyes on Jesus." If we look around at others, we are going to fumble and falter and fail as Landy did. Jesus is waiting at the end of the race to welcome us as victors (2 Tim. 4:6-8). If we keep our eyes on him, we will make it.

It is obvious that the picture portrayed in these opening verses of the 12th chapter of Hebrews is that of a long-distance (Marathon) race. But too few people have realized that this metaphor carries over to our text, verse 14.

The KJV says, "Follow peace." But the Greek verb is *dioko,* which means "pursue" (NASB). And it is in the present imperative of continuous action: "Keep on pursuing."

This verb *dioko* was used in classical Greek for an animal pursuing its prey. We might illustrate this.

Some years ago I was preaching at a church in Missouri. We were invited out to a farm home for Sunday dinner. While the meal was being prepared, I sauntered down by the barn.

Soon the pastor and the man of the place came down and joined me. The latter showed me his thoroughbred hunting hounds and then related to me what I want to share with you.

He said that sometimes on Saturday morning he would set his dogs loose. Barking excitedly, they would race out to the open field and woods.

After awhile their barking turned to baying, and he knew they were on the trail of a fox. Then the fox would lead them for a merry chase. He would circle back across his trail, and that would confuse them. He would cross a shallow creek, causing them to bark loudly as they lost the trail for a little while. The owner said to me: "I have actually sat down to milk my cow at five o'clock in the afternoon, and I would still hear those dogs baying on the track of that 'foxy' fox."

If we would pursue peace and holiness as persistently and perseveringly as a common hound dog, we would all succeed. What we need is *dogged* perseverance!

Our text suggests four propositions.

I. You can't pursue peace with people successfully unless you first make peace with God. Probably no thoughtful Christian would question that.

II. You can't *maintain* peace with God unless you *keep on pursuing* peace with people. The vertical relationship is primary. But the horizontal relationship is also essential.

The story is told of a couple sitting together on the buckboard seat of a farm wagon, as they drove along a country road. In front of them were two horses prancing along in perfect step on either side of the wagon tongue.

It so happened that things hadn't been going too well at home. Mary became rather pensive and sad. Finally she turned to her husband and said, "John, wouldn't it be wonderful if we could go through life together in perfect step, like those two horses."

John took one look at the horses and then growled out of the corner of his mouth: "We could if we had only one tongue between us like they have!"

Of course, the $64.00 question is: "Whose tongue is it going to be, his or hers?" And the answer is: "Both tongues must be on the altar, subservient to God's will and governed by divine love."

III. The third proposition is: You can't pursue holiness without getting sanctified wholly. We have known many individuals who, without any Wesleyan teaching, have been cleansed from all sin and filled with the Holy Spirit simply because they earnestly sought God's will with all their heart. Jesus said:

> "Blessed are those who hunger and thirst for righteousness, for they will be filled."

Paul declared: "It is God's will that you should be sanctified" (1 Thess. 4:3). In the same Epistle he defines what that sanctification is by praying that God "may sanctify you entirely" (NASB), "wholly" (KJV), or "through and through" (NIV). Entire sanctification is God's will for all His people.

Now we come to the fourth proposition:

IV. You can't keep sanctified without pursuing holiness all our life.

In effect the text says: "Keep on pursuing peace with all people, and keep on pursuing holiness of heart and life; if you don't, you will never see the Lord." If we want to spend a happy eternity in the light of His glorious presence, that is what we all must do. It is a lifelong pursuit. Failure to follow this pursuit can bring tragic results, here and hereafter.

Some years ago a pastor's wife in Florida shared with me a very moving experience. One day she held a service for women in a jail in the city where her husband pastored. At the close of her message, with everyone's eyes closed, she asked anyone who felt the need of prayer to lift her hand. A girl sitting in the back seat did so.

After the service was dismissed, the speaker made her way back to this girl. Taking her by the hand, she looked down into the face of a naturally rather pretty teenager and said: "Honey, you don't look like a girl who belongs in here."

Tears filled the girl's eyes, and she said: "No, I wasn't made for a place like this. You see, I've lived all my life in a Nazarene parsonage." When the pastor's wife asked what had happened, the girl shared this story with her.

She had lived a good life in high school but had never been sanctified wholly. One Sunday night her father preached a strong sermon on holiness and gave an invitation for seekers.

A lady stepped across the aisle and asked the girl if she would like to go to the altar and pray. The girl shook her head and said, "No, I'm all right." But the Holy Spirit was convicting her of her need.

Finally the girl turned around and left the church. She said that as she walked out the door she felt an awful sense that she wanted to have her fling. When we close the door of our heart to God we open it to Satan, and he will do his worst.

Later, she took up with a worthless girl in town. This one suggested, "Let's go to Florida!" And so they started out.

It wasn't long until they ran out of money and began thumbing for a ride. That night a man came along, stopped, and invited them to get in. They climbed into the front seat with him, our girl sitting next to the driver.

She said that as they rode on through the hours of the night they stopped at almost every tavern and went in for a drink. This girl, who was brought up in a Christian home and had never touched a drop of liquor, was drinking that night with a godless stranger. When we deliberately walk away from God we put ourselves on the devil's toboggan slide, and never dream how *fast* and how *far* we may go down the hill to our ruin!

In the early hours of the morning the man said to the girls, "Do you have any money?" They replied, "No; that's why we were hitchhiking."

The man cried out, "I've got to have a drink. If I don't, I'll die." What a pity!

Just then they saw a car parked beside the road. Its driver had become sleepy, so he had pulled over to the side, turned off the motor, and stretched out on the front seat—without locking the car doors!

The man with whom the girls were riding pulled over, yanked the other car door open, and demanded the billfold of the now wide-awake traveler. Instead of complying, the man jumped out of the car and started wrestling with his would-be robber. When the first man saw that he was getting the worst of the struggle, he stabbed the resisting man in the chest. Then he returned to his own car where the girls were waiting, and slumped over the steering wheel in a drunken stupor.

Soon a state patrolman came along, saw the bleeding body beside the road, stopped, and began to administer first aid. On his radio he called for an ambulance.

By this time the drunken driver was awakened by sirens blasting and bright lights shining. Glancing down, he saw the bloody knife in his hand. He slipped it to the girl beside him, saying: "Here, get this out of sight." She quickly hid it inside her dress.

When the victim was taken away in the ambulance, the police turned their attention to the other car still parked by the highway. They took the three passengers into the police station. There the bloody knife was found in the possession of the pastor's daughter. She was given a five-year sentence. Fortunately the victim lived. If he had died, she would have received life imprisonment.

The lady who related this told me: "The other day I visited the state penitentiary. The girl said to me: 'God has forgiven me and taken me back. I have gone on and gotten sanctified wholly.' Then with a wail in her voice she cried, 'But that doesn't keep me from having to spend five years behind the bars just for having my own way for a few hours.'"

Let me say to all who read this; you can't afford to have your own way. It costs too much. When the Lord asks you to surrender your will wholly to His will, say "Yes, Lord" and do it. You will never be sorry you did!

9

1 PETER
What Is a Holy Person?

Text: 1 Pet. 1:15-16

Introduction:

How does one become a holy person? Dr. A. B. Simpson, the founder of the Christian and Missionary Alliance, was one of the holiest men of his generation. How did it happen? He describes his crisis experience this way:

"The Lord Jesus revealed himself as a living and all-sufficient presence, and I learned for the first time that Christ had not saved us from future peril and left us to fight the battle of life as best we could; but He who had justified us was waiting to sanctify us, to enter into our spirit and substitute His strength, His holiness, His joy, His love, His faith, His power, for all our worthlessness, helplessness, and nothingness, and make it an actual living fact."

And Charles H. Spurgeon, one of Britain's greatest preachers and soul winners, once declared: "If I have won men to Christ, it has been because I have received the Holy Spirit."

We cannot be holy people until we have been filled with the Holy Spirit. It is His cleansing, sanctifying presence that makes us holy.

The Greek adjective *hagios,* "holy," occurs about 230 times in the New Testament. In the Septuagint, the Greek translation of the Old Testament made about 200 years before Christ, it is found nearly 500 times. This makes over 700 times that this word *holy* occurs in our Holy Bible.

In the New Testament this adjective is translated *holy* 161 times in the KJV. But also note that the word *saints* (61 times) is a translation of this same adjective in the plural. So "saints" are literally "holy ones." A holy God must have a holy people. A person is not a true saint unless he is a holy person.

The frequency of the word *holy* shows that holiness is a dominant theme in the Bible. In the Old Testament the term is applied largely to things, especially in the Pentateuch. The ancient Tabernacle had a holy place and a holy of holies, or most holy place, where God's presence dwelt. But in the New Testament it is primarily persons who are holy.

In response to the question "What Is a Holy Person?" three answers are considered.

I. A Holy Person Is One Who Is Set Apart to God

The verb *hagiazo,* "sanctify," is formed from the adjective *hagios,* "holy," and the letter *zeta,* which carries the causative effect. So it literally means "make holy." But it is generally recognized that often in the Old Testament the term *sanctify* has its minimal meaning of "set apart to God for sacred use."

If we are going to be holy people, the first thing we must do is to give ourselves completely to God—body, soul, and spirit. Unless we belong fully to Him, we are not really holy persons. And this is *our* decision; God cannot make it for us. We have to die to *self* in order to become fully alive to *God.* As long as we want to have our own way and do our own thing we cannot be holy persons. But if we are willing to consecrate ourselves completely to God, then He will sanctify us wholly, stamping us with the seal of His Holy Spirit, showing that we are now His property, belonging fully to Him.

This leads to the second answer in response to the question. It is this:

II. A Holy Person Is One Who Is Filled with the Spirit

It is only the indwelling presence of the Holy Spirit that can make *us* truly holy. We have to be emptied of self in order to be filled with himself.

This means first of all a crisis experience, as it was for the 120 disciples on the Day of Pentecost. They had tarried for about 10 days in the Upper Room, "joined together constantly in prayer" (Acts 1:14). They waited before the Lord, dying out to self, and consecrating their all to God. Finally they received the fiery baptism with the Holy Spirit, which Jesus had predicted in Acts 1:5. John the Baptist had foretold this when he said to his followers: "I baptize you with water for repentance. But after me will come one who is more powerful than I . . . He will baptize you with the Holy Spirit and with fire" (Matt. 3:11). This means a fiery baptism that would cleanse their hearts from all sin.

That is the *crisis.* But there must also be a *continuation.* In Eph. 5:18 Paul admonished his readers: "Be filled with the Spirit." Here the Greek verb is in the present tense of continuous action. So it literally means "Be continually filled with the Spirit." Only the Holy Spirit can *make* us holy and only He can *keep* us holy. It is His active, sanctifying presence in our hearts every day that enables us to be holy.

Now we come to the third answer:

III. A Holy Person Is One Who Is Living a Holy Life

Our text says: "Be holy in all you do." The KJV reads: "Be ye holy in all manner of conversation." It is true that in 1611 *conversation,* from the Latin, meant "manner of living." But it is now used in the narrower sense of "talking." The Greek word that Paul used here takes in all of life. Peter told his readers to be "holy in all you do." We are to be holy in every area of our lives. "All you do" takes in not only our words but also our attitudes and actions. We are to live holy lives every day in every way.

The basic meaning of holiness is purity. A holy life is a pure life. That means that no hint of immorality is to be tolerated in the Christian's life. In a world that is now flooded with pornography, we must be very careful what we look at and listen to. Holy people cannot be too careful at this point. We are all human, and we live in bodies that still have their physical, God-given appetites. So we must guard our lives every day against evil influences around us, and we must keep our thoughts pure.

A further word needs to be said at this point. A favorite trick of the devil is to sit on one shoulder and whisper an unclean thought into our minds—then slip around to the other shoulder and accusingly say: "See, you are not sanctified! If you were, you wouldn't have had such a thought!"

We might also describe it another way. In a world such as we live in today it is almost impossible never to have a momentary thought that we regret. But thoughts of evil are not necessarily evil thoughts. They are not that unless and until we entertain them and begin to enjoy them. It has well been said: "You can't keep birds from flying over your head, but you can keep them from building nests in your hair." It's when we *harbor* bad thoughts that we get into serious trouble.

This leads to the idea that "bad thoughts" may not necessarily be related to what we think of as immoral. In God's sight unkind, unloving thoughts are *bad* thoughts. We must not entertain them, but rather we should quickly expel them, before they affect our attitudes and perhaps our words.

A new area now opens up to us for answering the question: "What is a holy person?" It is simply this: A holy person is a loving person. Holiness means godliness, or godlikeness. And the Bible declares: "God is love" (1 John 4:8, 16). If we are not loving, we are not godly, and so we are not holy.

This is a very important point. If our hearts are filled with the Holy Spirit, they are filled with love. And we must be sure that this love is dominating our lives—not only our outward actions but also our inner attitudes and thoughts. The only way to live a holy life is to ask God to help us show a loving attitude at all times. No matter what anyone does or says *to* us, or *about* us, we must love that person and *pray* for that one. In this way we keep our hearts pure and holy, regardless of what others do.

In conclusion I should like to give my own personal testimony. I was brought up in a very godly Quaker home. We had family worship twice a day and went to church—in horse and carriage seven miles each way—every Sunday morning and evening, as well as to midweek prayer meeting. And this in spite of the fact that on our dairy farm the cows had to be milked between five and six o'clock, morning and evening every day, including Sunday.

I had a childhood experience of loving the Lord. But during my first two years in a large public high school I lost out spiritually. I was never guilty of outwardly doing anything contrary to the very high standards of our church or home. But in my heart I wanted to have my own way, and that means I was a sinner. You are not a sinner because of what you *do* outside, but because of what you *are* inside. As has often been said: When a ship's in the sea, it's safe; but when the sea's in the ship, it's sunk. And I had self-will inside. I was sunk.

Fortunately, my parents decided to send me away to a Quaker academy for my last two years of high school. Soon after I arrived there, in a Bible study class on Friday afternoon, I knelt beside my schoolroom chair, confessed I was nothing but a lowdown sinner, and asked Jesus to come into my heart as my Savior. He did, and my soul was flooded with joy. It was joy unspeakable and full of glory.

The next Monday morning in chapel the Holy Spirit convicted me of my need to be sanctified wholly. I knelt at the altar and asked God to fill my heart with His Holy Spirit.

This time there was a somewhat prolonged struggle before I could submit my will fully to God's will. I was faced with one thing that I felt I couldn't do.

I thought I had placed everything on the altar, to let God have His way with all my life. And then someone confronted me with a question that shook me: "Suppose God should ask you to preach on the Pullman car when you are going home next spring; would you do it?" (At that time I rode Pullman, with Dad paying the bills. When I paid the bills, I rode jalopy!)

I remembered that train ride out from Boston to Indianapolis. All the people in that Pullman car were nice, cultured, high-class adults. I could imagine getting up in front of that sophisticated group and starting to preach. No way! You'd never find this proud young Yankee from New England making a fool of himself doing that! I struggled at the altar in bitter tears.

Finally I became so desperate to be filled with the Spirit, that I cried out: "Yes, Lord, I'll do it if it kills me!" In that moment I died to self, and came fully alive in Christ. Emptied of self, I was filled with himself. I was as happy as a bird, and just as free.

I have made plenty of mistakes since that day, November 6, 1922. But I can honestly say that I never once have said no to God. Always my prayer has been: "Not my will, but yours be done" (Luke 22:42). That means perfect peace—and "a holy person." Now I could sing:

Peace! peace! wonderful peace,
Coming down from the Father above!
Sweep over my spirit forever, I pray,
In fathomless billows of love.

10

1 JOHN
Walking in the Light

"Walking in the beautiful light of God" is clearly portrayed in 1 John 1:7: "But if we walk in the light, as he is in the light, we have fellowship with one another, and the blood of Jesus, his Son, purifies us from all sin." The Greek word here is the same as that translated "all" in verse 9—"all unrighteousness."

What verse 7 declares is that if we walk in the light the blood of Jesus purifies (or "cleanses") us from *all* sin. That includes the sinful nature (inbred sin), as well as our sinful acts.

The main emphasis in 1 John is on "love." The Greek noun *agape* occurs 116 times in the New Testament. It is found most frequently (18 times) in the rather short First Epistle of John. It is the key word of this letter written by the beloved apostle in his old age. Incidentally, the Greek verb *agapao* ("love") is found most frequently in the Gospel of John (37 times) and his First Epistle (28 times)—65 out of the 142 times it occurs in the New Testament.

The fourth chapter, where we find the significant expression "perfect love," deserves special attention. In verse 12 John declares that "if we love one another, God lives in us and his love is made complete in us." Verse 17 says: "Love is made complete among us so that we will have confidence on the day of judgment." Finally, verse 18 tells us: "There is no fear in love. But perfect love drives out fear, because fear has to do with punishment. The one who fears is not made perfect in love."

The verb for "made complete" (vv. 12, 17) is *teleioo*, which comes from *telos*, "end." So it literally means "bring to an end," or "make complete." The adjective *perfect* (v. 18) is *teleia*, which means "complete" or "perfect." And *made perfect* (v. 18) is the same verb (slightly different form) as that translated "made complete" in verses 12 and 17. It does seem to us that it would be more consistent for the NIV to have "made perfect" in those two verses (cf. KJV, NASB).

As we have noted previously, "God is love" (1 John 4:8, 16), and the Holy Spirit is God. So when our hearts are "filled with the Holy Spirit" (Acts 2:4), they are filled with love—or, as John says, "made perfect in love." So the Spirit-filled Christian has the experience of "perfect love." John Wesley declared that his favorite designation of entire sanctification was "Christian perfection." In fact, his main book on the subject of sanctification is titled *Plain Account of Christian Perfection*.

One of the leading evangelical New Testament scholars of our day made an interesting observation. He wrote that for the Christian church Martin Luther rediscovered Paul, while John Wesley rediscovered John. Luther emphasized, especially from Romans, justification by faith. We are not saved by keeping the Mosaic law or church ordinances, but only by faith in Jesus Christ as Savior and Lord. Wesley, two centuries later, moved on to an emphasis on perfect love. And so the modern holiness movement came into existence in the 19th century and flourishes today. Of course Paul also gives considerable emphasis to the doctrine and experience of entire sanctification, as we have seen.

What has been emphasized throughout this book is that if we are going to be "filled with the Spirit" we must be "purified from all sin," including the "sinful nature" (carnality). In closing we should like to share one of the most vivid pictures of "the carnal mind" (as Paul designates it) to be found anywhere in literature. It occurs in C. S. Lewis's striking book *The Great Divorce.*

C. S. Lewis saw a man standing nearby, with a red lizard on his shoulder. This red lizard was a type of our inbred sin, or "sinful nature."

The lizard was talking into the man's ear. Lewis could tell by the look on the man's face that he was very much annoyed by the presence of the red lizard.

Just then Lewis saw "the Flaming Spirit"—his very appropriate designation for the Holy Spirit (see Matt. 3:11)—come near and say to the man, "Would you like me to make him quiet?"

"Yes!"

"Then I will kill him."

"No, I think the gradual process is better."

The Flaming Spirit answered: "The gradual process is of no use at all."

The man countered: "Some other day, perhaps."

The Flaming Spirit answered: "There is no other day." What a profound truth! God's Word declares: "Now is the day of salvation" (2 Cor. 6:2).

Then the man exclaimed: "Get back! You're burning me."

The Flaming Spirit replied: "I never said it wouldn't hurt you."

Then the man suggested: "Let me go back and get an opinion from my doctor. I'll come again the first moment I can."

Once more C. S. Lewis puts in the mouth of the Flaming Spirit a very striking statement: "This moment contains all moments." Each moment is a segment of eternity and can have eternal significance.

Then the man whined: "Why didn't you kill it without asking me?"

The Flaming Spirit answered: "I cannot kill it against your will. Have I your permission?"

"Do what you like; God help me."

The man screamed as the Burning One closed His crimson grip on the lizard, twisted it, and flung it dead at his feet.

Then C. S. Lewis writes these words: "There are only two kinds of people in the end: those who say to God, 'Thy will be done,' and those to whom God says, *'Thy* will be done'"— and that means hell, here on earth and forever in outer darkness.

Have you said that final, full yes to God: "Not my will, but Yours be done"? If you haven't, I would urge you right now to get down on your knees and say an everlasting "No!" to self and an everlasting "Yes!" to God. Then believe Him to sanctify you through and through.

CHAPTER FIVE

GRANDMOTHER

WHEN HOUND woke the next morning, Grandmother was stirring the ashes of the fire, holding a stick in her long, slender fingers. Her hair was rust and gold, like autumn leaves. Her eyes were as dark as coals and her lips curiously red.

"They're here," she said. "They're waiting for you."

"Who?" he asked, rubbing his eyes.

"You'll have to ask them," she said. "They've been very respectful, brought the proper gifts. They know the old ways." It was often hard to work out what Grandmother was talking about, and today she seemed more oblique than usual. He reckoned she might be referring to the people from Ophion.

Her fingers lifted, and he saw she had scratched a pattern there. He also saw that her fingers were stained with blood just past her knuckles.

"My valley," she said. "The mountains around, you see?"

He nodded. "I've seen maps before, in the village."

She traced her finger through a series of ridges and flatlands, until finally she passed beyond where he had been in his travels.

"Here," she said. "A mountain with three peaks stepping down, tallest, middle, lowest."

"What about it?"

She sighed. "I have loved you," she said. "It has been so long. I nearly remember who I am, but now you must go. They have paid the price."

"You sold me?" he said.

"No. I only grant them the chance to speak to you, here, where you are still safe. You can choose to refuse them and remain with me."

"Well, then I shall," he said.

"No," she replied. "You will go with them."

"But if I have the choice—"

She placed her hand on his shoulder.

"Talk to them," she said.

SOOT FOUND them first, cawing and circling in the dark morning sky, but moments later Hound heard the racket of their horses and voices pitched low. They were in the hollow just inside Grandmother's forest. It was the second time he had ever known someone other than himself to cross the boundary. The first had been a single man, four years ago.

He had not survived.

Hound circled around so he could see them from the hill above, Rose shadowing him a few yards away. There were twenty of them and more than twice as many horses. Three of them wore armor of a kind he had never seen before—it was made of metal sheet and covered their limbs as well as their chests. None of them had their helmets on, however; not at the moment. Against his sling they

THE
BASILISK
THRONE

GREG KEYES

TITAN BOOKS

The Basilisk Throne

Print edition ISBN: 9781789095487
E-book edition ISBN: 9781789095494

Published by Titan Books
A division of Titan Publishing Group Ltd
144 Southwark Street, London SE1 0UP
www.titanbooks.com

First edition: April 2023
1 3 5 7 9 10 8 6 4 2

A CIP catalogue record for this title is available from the British Library.

Printed and bound in the United Kingdom by CPI Group (UK) Ltd,
Croydon, CR0 4YY.

For Sandra Baxter

THE BATTLE
OF THE EXPIRY

988 E.N.

"HARD ABOUT!" Captain Salemon shouted, as half of their prow disintegrated into a cloud of wooden shards. Sailors fell screaming as splinters pierced them. As Alastor watched, his friend Danyel covered his eyes with both hands, stumbling as blood leaked through his fingers.

The *Laros* rocked under a second impact, so jarring that Alastor nearly lost his grip on the rigging. Flames erupted, spreading across the deck like a liquid.

"Christ of Ophion," Jax yelped. Alastor saw his fellow navior holding on by one hand, dangling twenty feet above the deck below. He reached out and grabbed Jax by his shirt, pulling him closer so he could double his grip.

"Captain, if we turn, we cannot engage," Lieutenant Captain La Treille snapped. "Our orders—"

"We are two hundred yards from being at the outside of our

range," Salemon returned. "We'll be fish food long before we cover the distance."

Even Alastor, as green as he was, could see the truth in that. Every ship on their line had been hit, and several were sinking, while the Drehhu vessels remained untouched in the distance. Whatever demonic weapons they were using, they had a far greater range then the spear-flinging quilaines with which the *Laros* was armed. The fleet was being chewed to pieces, and they hadn't yet fired a shot.

"They *are* demons," Jax said.

"Come on," Alastor said. "We've got to get the sails up."

They were going against the wind, so they had dropped sail and put the rowers to work. The ship was turning, but very slowly.

"Ah, merde," Jax said. "The captain's put us broadside."

The mainmast exploded in flame; what was left of it went up like a torch. The ship lurched as her babord side was slammed repeatedly by the invisible weapons of the Drehhu. La Treille twisted at the waist and kept turning, as his body tore apart and caught fire at the same time.

"We're done," Jax said. He groaned, and Alastor saw his friend had a splinter of the mast as long as an arm sticking out of his chest. Then Jax let go and plummeted to the flaming deck.

As the ship foundered, Alastor clung to the rigging. When it tipped to the side, he let go and fell into the sea. The Drehhu flames ran across the surface of the water. Swimming furiously as the fire swept toward him, he felt heavier with each stroke as the woolen clothing that had kept him warm during their cold passage to this battle became a sodden weight pulling him down. His breath rasped in his chest. His arms and legs stopped burning with exertion and began to grow numb for the chill in the water.

Alastor's head dipped below the surface and salt stung his nose. If not for the many hours of his boyhood spent swimming, he would already be sunken in the gray depths. These were not the warm, sunny waters of the Coste de Sucre, however. He had escaped the fire, but even so he knew he didn't have long to live.

He spied some floating wreckage and bore toward it, grasping with fingers he could no longer feel, and pulling his arms around it. It wasn't much, not enough to pull himself fully out of the water, but it kept him afloat. He rested a moment, eyes closed, drawing in breath before opening them once more to look around.

IN THE distance, it looked as if the whole fleet was burning. Forty-five ships of war, turned to scrap in under an hour. Against all odds, a few had managed to come into range before succumbing to the enemy weapons, but so far as he could see, not one of the Drehhu vessels had been damaged. He was hardly surprised. They had no masts and were armored in metal.

The fleet of Ophion had never had a chance, here on the open sea.

The flames on the waves flickered and died away until only a few ghostly blue vapors remained. It was strangely beautiful, and then they too were gone, leaving only the iron-colored swells.

Another survivor began swimming his way.

"Do you mind?" the fellow asked, gasping as he drew near. He was a freckle-faced man with auburn hair.

"Come aboard," Alastor said. "I'm Alastor Nevelon, from the *Laros*." He helped the man find his grip on the flotsam and then waited for him to gather enough air to speak again.

"Henri Vallet," the other navior finally said. "Late of the *Delphis*."

"Charmed," Alastor said. "With the two of us pushing this thing, we might be able to join up with that bit of debris over there." He gestured.

"Ah, and have a proper boat," Vallet said. "I'm for that." They set out, kicking hard and navigating their piece of wreckage, and had some luck. Their prize was part of a mast that had some rope on it. It seemed like hours before they managed to lash together enough of a raft that they were able to draw themselves out of the water, and the overcast sky was little help in telling time. Once above the life-leaching sea they both sat silently, rubbing swollen hands. Alastor had torn out three nails, but didn't feel it yet due to the cold.

"Where from, Nevelon?" Vallet asked, after a time.

"Mesembria," he replied. "A place called Port Bellship."

Vallet nodded. "On the Coste de Sucre. Nice little place."

"And you?"

"Ophion Magne," the man said. "From the city. Not the nice part of it, though."

They fell silent. Other survivors could be seen, and more could be heard. Alastor turned his head slowly, surveying the horizon in all directions. The Drehhu ships were visible amongst the ruins of the center of the fleet, but none yet headed their way.

To the west, there was no horizon, only a strange grayness, like a wall of cloud.

"That's it, isn't it?"

"The Expiry," Vallet confirmed.

"We never had a chance," Alastor sighed. "What madness drove the admiral to this?"

"This wasn't the plan," Vallet said. "You must know that. The plan was to slip up into their port of Agath, and launch the assault in the harbor. We would have had twice their number, plus the advantage of surprise. That's why we swung out so far—so close to the edge of the world—to avoid being noticed until we were there. But the Drehhu found out and met us here, with our backs to the Expiry, so we had no choice but to fight."

"I hadn't heard any of that," Alastor said.

"Only the officers knew," Vallet replied.

"You're an officer?" Alastor stared at him. He wasn't wearing a coat or hat. "Sir," he added.

"Does it matter now?" Vallet said. "Shall I be captain of our little craft, for as long as it lasts? Be easy, Nevelon." They fell silent for a time, then Vallet spoke. "Tell me about Port Bellship. Did you grow up there?"

Alastor nodded. "My family has a sugar plantation."

"Really? And you chose to join the Navy rather than stay home and drink rum?"

"I thought I might see something of the world. Serve my emperor. Later, perhaps become a merchant sailor." He glanced at the Expiry. He was certain now.

The current was taking them toward it.

Vallet noticed. "Yes," he said, acknowledging the obvious. He didn't sound afraid, or even worried. Just tired. "This is as close as I've ever been."

"They say it cuts the world in half."

"It runs from farthest north to farthest south, that much we know to be true," Vallet said, "but whether or not the other half of the world lies beyond it, who can say?" He nodded toward the gray wall of mist that stretched as far as they could see in either direction. "No one who has ever crossed into that has ever come back. It might well be the edge of the world. It might be a wall between us and Hell."

"I fear we shall find out," Alastor said, although he also felt too exhausted to properly dread their fate.

Vallet glanced toward the Drehhu ships.

Two were moving in their direction.

"We know what the alternative is," Vallet said. "If the Drehhu do not kill us, they will enslave us."

Up ahead, from the direction of the Expiry, Alastor heard a single unholy shriek, followed quickly by another, then more, until there was a chorus of them.

"That doesn't sound promising."

The wall of mist loomed over them, filling their vision so that it was impossible to tell how distant it was, or how near. Not far off were four naviors on another makeshift raft. They vanished into it, and he expected to hear them scream, but there was no sound. A moment later he thought he heard something, but it might have been his imagination. The sky grew darker, and the approaching Drehhu ships became shadows in the distance.

They heard more shrieks of despair, and then other sounds— deep, stuttering clicks and weird, glissando wails, rising and falling in pitch from a high keening to tones so low he felt more than heard them. And a faint shushing, like an inconstant wind but also like distant whispering in an unknown language.

As full night came on, he thought he saw faint, shifting colors in the darkness.

"When will it happen?" Alastor asked.

"Perhaps we are already within," Vallet replied.

"It does not feel different." But even as he said it, he began to experience a prickling on his flesh, and his heart beat faster. It felt as something was shining on the side of him—the one that seemed to be facing the Expiry. A light his eyes could not perceive.

There was another strange noise: a grinding, churning sort of sound.

"Damn!" Vallet suddenly shouted. "Behind us."

Alastor turned. He saw lights and the outline of a ship. A Drehhu ship. The awful noise was coming from it. A lantern of some sort turned toward them, and the beam fell on their makeshift raft. The enemy ship began to turn, then came directly toward them.

In that light, Alastor could see the Expiry, no more than ten yards away.

"We could swim," he said. "Deny them their prize."

"A slave can escape," Vallet said. "He can escape and return to his home and drink rum in the evenings." He nodded at the wall of mist. "From that, there is no return."

Alastor nodded. He could see figures moving on the ship now. Not human. Bigger, with broader shoulders. They had four limbs like men, but those were long and spindly, and they made him think more of spiders than of people.

"A slave can escape," Alastor agreed.

BOOK ONE

THE

COST OF

SUGAR

CHAPTER ONE

AMMOLITE

1009 E.N.

THE FIRST time Ammolite looked in a mirror, she was sixteen.

She vomited.

Ammolite was a slave. She did not remember her mother selling her, but Veulkh assured her that it had happened.

"A silver bar and a necklace of glass gems," he informed her. "That was your price."

Of course, that was after he began talking to her.

Her earliest memories were of wandering the opalescent, faintly glowing halls of his manse, of standing alone on stone balconies, traveling her gaze over the snow-covered peaks that surely held up the sky. Down the almost sheer rock face into which the manse was built, to the mysterious green valley far below. She left bits of food on the balcony for the birds, and over time some would take their treats from her fingers. She fancied they were her friends and gave them names.

A woman came each day to feed her, read to her, and later teach her to read, but Ammolite never knew her name. No sentiment developed between them. The woman did her job, and hardly spoke a word to her that was not written in a book. Once Ammolite could read passably, the woman showed her the library, and thereafter did not come again.

A new woman brought her meals and did not speak at all. None of the other servants talked to her, either, and she came to realize that some of them were not even capable of speech.

She read and she stared from the balconies, moving through her world almost like a ghost, and though she knew she had a master— and that his name was Veulkh—she never saw him.

Until, one day, she did.

MOUNTED ON a wall in her room was a calendar, a round mechanical thing of brass and crystal that counted off the days of her life. Once she came to understand it, she knew on a given day that she was—for instance—six years and seventy-five days of age. She did not often consult it, for each day was like any other, and the number of them hardly seemed to matter.

But one morning the calendar, clicking along as usual, suddenly belled a single, beautiful tone. She was awake already, and she stared at the device in astonishment. This was something different, something that had never happened before. It filled her with an unexpected sense of hope and anticipation.

She was exactly sixteen years old.

Before she could rise and dress, a small, hunched woman she had never seen before entered the room, bearing a gown of black silk.

"You will wear this," the woman said.

The gown had unfamiliar fastenings but the woman helped her put it on. Up until then, Ammolite's clothing had been simple shifts she pulled on over her head, so she did not know much about clothes, but the dress seemed far too big for her. It piled on the floor and tried to slip from her shoulders. She felt lost in it.

Then the woman led her through the manor into halls she had never seen, to a room with a table large enough to accommodate twice a dozen people but which was set with only two places. At one of these places sat Veulkh.

She was a little surprised at how young he looked. She knew he was a sorcerer, and from her reading she knew that it took many years to become a master of those arts. From some of the things she had overheard the servants say, she thought he must be very old indeed, but his dark hair and beard lacked any hint of silver, and his face was handsome and young.

And yet she still did not like to look upon it. There was something there that bothered her.

The woman led her to her seat. Like the dress, it seemed too large.

"Ammolite," he said, absently. She wasn't sure he was speaking to her at first, but then he faced her directly. Though his features were composed, almost serene, his eyes were peculiar, as if he was looking beyond or perhaps *into* her.

The woman brought each of them a glass of something red.

"I named you that," Veulkh said, sipping at the red liquid. "Ammolite." Unsure what to do, she took her glass and tasted its contents. It was strange and harsh, like fruit juice but with something a little spoiled in it.

When she did not say anything, he crooked a finger at her.

"You may speak," he said.

"I did not know you named me," she said.

"You had another name, before I purchased you," he said. "I don't remember what it was." He smiled. "It hardly matters, does it?"

"I suppose not, Master," she replied.

He took another drink of the red stuff.

"This is called wine," he told her. "Vin in the language of Ophion. Nawash, in Modjal. It has other names. It is made from grapes."

"Is it made by magic?" she asked.

"Yes," he said. "A kind of alchemy is involved."

She took another tentative swallow. It still didn't taste good.

"I mentioned Ophion and Modjal," he said. "Do you know what I was referring to?"

"Ophion is an empire," she said. "Its capital is named Ophion Magne. It is said that a god by that name died and was buried there. They have an emperor and a council of savants. They are famous for textiles—"

"And Modjal?"

"Another empire, southeast of Ophion. Also with a capital of the same name, also said to be the resting place of an ancient god. Their emperor is known as the Qho—"

"Very good," he said. "You've been reading the books I provided you."

"Yes, Master."

He nodded approvingly.

"Do you understand, Ammolite, what it is to be a slave?"

"It means that you own me," she replied.

"That is correct," Veulkh said. "Like this wine, and the glass it is poured in. If I wish to hurl it against the wall and shatter it, that is entirely my decision. The glass and the wine have no say in the matter."

"I understand, Master."

He drained the rest of his drink in a single gulp and then cocked his arm back to dash it against the wall—but then he smiled and settled the glass back on the table. The woman came to refill it from a crystal pitcher.

"Have you ever wondered why you are here?"

She had, but she did not say so. She shook her head and drank a little more of the wine.

"You are here," he said, "as any slave is, because there are one or more tasks I require of you."

"I understand, Master," she said, "but I do not know what they are."

"Finish your wine, and I will show you," he said.

He watched in silence as she drank. It became easier as she went along. A sort of warmth crept over her, and her nervousness began to fade.

There is magic in this, she thought.

She wished he would talk more. She liked being spoken to.

"I've read about Velesa, as well," she attempted. "That is where we are, isn't it?"

"Who told you that?" he asked, a bit sharply.

"No one," she said, "but your books are mostly in the language of Velesa, and your servants speak it—and that nation is known for high mountains."

"You're quite certain none of my servants mentioned it?"

"I'm certain, Master."

"Well, you are mistaken," he said. "That is not where we are." He settled back, but a little frown remained on his face. He gestured for her to finish the wine. When she was done, he signaled to the woman, who left the room. Then he stood.

"Come, Ammolite," he said.

She followed him, feeling a bit sluggish and clumsy. Her head was a little whirly. He led her through a door and into a room furnished mostly in red, and sat her upon a large bed. Then he knelt before her and took her hands. It was such a shock her first instinct was to pull away—hardly anyone had ever touched her, and she never touched anyone. She didn't like it. His fingers felt warm, even hot, but they were gentle, and so she tried to breathe slowly, to bear it until it was over.

He placed her palms on his temples.

"Close your eyes," he said. "Look. See her."

She didn't know what he meant, but she closed her eyes. At first she saw nothing other than darkness, the backs of her eyelids, but gradually something appeared, a mist, a light.

The light became a face, a woman's face. She had dark eyes and pale skin, and her hair was as black as smoke. She trembled; it felt like a thousand insects were crawling upon her skin—and under it.

"There," he said. "Open your eyes."

She did so and found herself staring into his face.

"Orra," he murmured. His eyes had changed. They seemed more alive, full of some barely contained emotion. As she stared, he began to weep.

"You must say you love me," he said.

"I-I, l-love you," she stammered, suddenly more afraid than ever. Then he pushed his lips onto hers. She felt a rush of claustrophobia, as if she couldn't move her limbs, and tried to shove him away. Her body felt… bigger. Different. Not hers, somehow.

"You must say I please you," he said. "You must."

He was touching her now, touching her everywhere. His fingers were still gentle, but she wanted to scream, to get away.

"I have waited so long, Orra," he whispered into her ear. "You've been gone so long, but I kept you, kept you…" He put his lips on her again, rougher this time, and on her neck and chest. He pressed her back on the bed as he pushed up her dress.

WHEN IT was over, she still did not know what had happened, but she was sore and sick. She cried, but he kept speaking to her, telling her to say she loved him and how pleased she was. It was almost as if he was begging, and so she did, through the sobs.

"You don't understand, do you?"

"No."

"Go there." He pointed. "Turn the mirror around."

She did so, happy to be out of the bed, away from him. He had pointed at a wooden frame, mounted on a swivel. She had read about mirrors, had caught faint glimpses of herself in water basins and the polished marble in some of the halls, but had never seen one. She turned the frame.

Ammolite had milky hair, and a small, narrow face. She thought her eyes were pale blue or maybe even white, but what she saw in the mirror was the woman with the black hair. The dress was not loose on her; she filled it with all the curves of the grown women who had attended her. When Ammolite moved her hand, the dark-tressed woman in the glass did the same.

And then she vomited.

Over on the bed, Veulkh laughed at her.

When she was done, trembling, she looked back up at the

mirror, and the woman was gone, replaced by a sixteen-year-old girl in a dress far too large for her.

I want to die, she thought.

It would not be the last time.

SHE DIDN'T know the word for what had happened to her, and there was no one to tell her. The books in the library contained information on a wide variety of subjects, but nothing concerning what that thing was and why he put it in her.

As the calendar in her room ticked by her days and her birthdays— seventeen, eighteen, nineteen, twenty—she came to endure it. She became better and better at saying the things he wanted her to say, in the tone of voice he wanted. She learned to make it go more quickly.

In time, he stopped instructing her entirely, but instead gazed at her as if she were the only thing in the world that mattered. He told her again and again how he loved her, but she did not really know what that meant. She finally found a book that described the forms of "love." One of them—eros—seemed to involve the things he did to her body with his. Another sort of love—pragma—seemed to explain the way he behaved after he was done with that.

It was in those moments that he spoke to her of things he and Orra had shared, long ago, the countries they had visited, places he would take her again. She realized that, in Veulkh's mind, she had become two entirely different people—Ammolite and Orra. Sometimes she feared the same separation was happening in her own mind.

As Ammolite she could not bear his touch. It was easier to pretend she was Orra when he took her to the bed.

Except for one thing.

Orra—whoever and whenever she was—must have loved him as he loved her. Ammolite had only the mistiest notion of what love might be, but she knew she did not love Veulkh. She was, in fact, not even fond of him, as the books described it, no matter how embarrassingly sincere his pledges of devotion to her were.

There was another change, as well, and she took full advantage of it. Each night she was Orra and slept in his chambers, but by day—as Ammolite—she could go where she wished within the seemingly endless manse.

Besides the bedroom and dining room, Veulkh's suite contained a kitchen with a balcony and a view of the mountains. Adjoining it was a steam room and bath tiled in turquoise and polished red coral depicting dolphins and sea serpents. What interested her most, however, was the spiral stair that led upward. Treading it, she discovered Veulkh's library, which made for much more interesting reading than her own.

There were tomes on alchemy and thaumaturgy, venoms and vitriol, the humors of the universe and the human body, the atomies that dwell in living blood. Many of the books concerned weather and the nature of it, and of the world, its mountains and rivers and seas. Then there were the volumes written in scripts she could not read, but whose illustrations suggested they might be books of spells.

The first time Veulkh discovered her in the library, she thought she might be punished, but he hardly seemed to notice her. As she had once felt like a ghost, she had now *become* a ghost to him, for when she was Ammolite he hardly seemed to notice her at all.

One day, not long after her twentieth birthday, she decided to see how invisible she truly was, to discover if she could find the exit from the manse and simply walk away.

But if there was a way out, she never found it.

So she continued her self-education. She tried to prise out the meanings of the cryptic symbols in the spellbooks. She searched for some explanation of how Veulkh changed her into Orra, but found nothing except that transformation was one of the most difficult and dangerous of magicks.

IT TOOK her two years to find the book, the thing for which she had been looking without knowing exactly what she was seeking. By that time, she had taught herself a pair of the obscure languages in which many of the texts were written. It was a treatise on synapses, the locations where the powers of the world crossed or converged. The most powerful were natural, but they could also be created.

Soon after her first night with him, Veulkh took her to see his conjury, where he did his most powerful magics. She was certain it was one such synapse.

From the book she learned of another sort of synapsis, one each sorcerer fashioned for themselves. It was sometimes referred to as a "heart" or "core," and was something like a key used to unlock the other powers of the world, an intermediary between will and practice.

That heart was also a vulnerability, for once it had been made, the sorcerer could not survive without it.

If she could find Veulkh's heart…

She hardly dared think it at first. The book didn't describe what such a thing would look like, but a few weeks after reading the book, she began to search. Carefully.

Veulkh's conjury was above the library, a vast space carved deep into the living stone of the mountain, but with one face open to the wind. The floor was concave, and so smooth that she nearly slipped the first time she set foot upon it. Besides the stairway entrance there were two additional portals—one quite large, the other of a size with those throughout the manse. Both were always locked.

Sometimes she watched him work. It was never the same twice. At times he surrounded himself with dark fumes and sang in a guttural language. On other occasions, he drank potions, traced symbols on the floor, or sketched them in the air with a burning wand. Sometimes he made no preparation other than to walk to the center of the room and stand silently.

Whatever his behavior, the hair pricked up on the nape of her neck and she felt strange tastes in the back of her throat. Light and color became weird, and faint noises sounded within her skull. It frightened her, but she was also strangely drawn to it.

She also began to see what it did to him, how each time afterward he was both more and less than he had been before. Sometimes he lay in a daze, neither truly awake nor asleep, twitching at things she did not see. When this happened, however, Kos, the captain of his ravens, was always near, along with four or five other guards. The ravens dressed in red, umber, and black-checked doublets and were armed with sword and dagger.

They were not slaves. He paid them in gold.

At times the stairwell door was locked. On many of the occasions when he was rendered weak, she could not see what he did. On those days, the very stone of the mountain shook, as if thunder had been loosed inside of it. At first it had alarmed her, but eventually she learned to accept it as a natural way of things.

"Why do you do it?" she asked him one night, when she wore Orra's face. She had drunk more wine than usual and felt talkative.

"Because I can," he replied. For a moment, she wasn't sure he knew what she was asking, but then he rolled on his side and looked her in the eyes. "Princes beg for my services," he said. "Emperors fling gold at my feet, and yet I am beholden to no one."

"What of the Cryptarchia?" she asked.

An expression of impatience began to inform his features. "What do you know of the Cryptarchia?" he asked.

"That it's something like a guild," she replied. "A sorcerous guild."

"That clucking bunch of hens." He sighed. "I condescend to follow their rubrics when it suits me, but I long ago rose above them. I am my own. The cryptarchs—politicians, librarians, and their strigas-sniffing bitches. It can hardly be named sorcery, what they practice. There are very few of my kind, Orra. I am one of the last."

"But there are others?"

"A few," he replied. "None so powerful as me. And now we shall speak no more of this."

She knew his moods, and so pressed no further. For several months things went on as they always had.

Then the calendar struck her twenty-first birthday.

CHAPTER TWO

CHRYSANTHE

COSTE DE SUCRE, MESEMBRIA

1014 E.N.

CHRYSANTHE KNEW Lucien was going to kiss her.

A zephyr soughed through the sugar cane fields that rolled to the right and down from the hilltop path, stirring the curls of her golden hair. A flamboyance of flamingos rose through a saffron haze, drawing their silhouettes across the cinnamon and indigo clouds mounded on the horizon. Pale green sprites flitted in the jagged fronds of the palm forest bordering the left side of the trail. The hem of her periwinkle gown brushed softly against the grass.

It seemed as if all the world was in a state of pleasant agitation.

And then they stopped walking.

Lucien was taller, so he had to bend. It gave her time to turn her face, so his lips landed on her cheek. He paused for a moment, his brown eyes peering uncertainly, and then abruptly straightened.

"I'm sorry," he said. "I suppose I wasn't thinking."

"I suspect you were doing a great deal of thinking."

She smiled, to soften it.

He folded his arms.

"It's just, the time we've spent together—when you asked me to escort you…"

"But I didn't, Lucien," she said. "You asked to accompany me. By the gate, as I was leaving."

A little furrow appeared on his forehead, and she thought again how handsome he was—pretty, almost, with his high cheekbones and aquiline nose. Although he was only twenty-five years of age, the line of his cinnamon hair was already receding from his brow, yet it lent him some needed gravity. As always, he was dressed fashionably—today in a canary shirt, a cravat of fawn ribbon, and a redingote of the same color. He held in his hands a small-brimmed bicorn hat.

"Yes," he said. "I suppose that's true—but really, how could I allow a lady to go solitary into the countryside?"

"You are gallant," she said, "and I am happy to have your company. Only… behave."

Lucien smiled: nervously, she thought. He was an entirely affable character, intelligent and well-read. She enjoyed their conversations. Of good birth, he was lately from distant, fabulous Ophion, an investor in her father's enterprises on an extended stay to learn how the sugar business was run. Quite different from the local characters who called on her.

A breath of fresh air, at least at first. And her mother adored him, with her eye always turned toward noble connections to lift the family from its mercantile roots.

Chrysanthe turned from the large path onto a smaller one that wound off through the palms.

"It is getting late," Lucien said. "The sun is nearly gone under. Perhaps we should turn back."

"Only a little further," she said. "It's been a long time since I've come this way. There's an old chapel just ahead. It's quite beautiful, especially at dusk."

"A proper chapel, you mean, or some old native collection of rocks?"

"Well, you can judge it for yourself."

They walked a few more paces.

"This seems like a dreadful idea," he said as they moved further from the fields and into the thickening forest. "We might become lost. Or some wild animal—"

"You have your sword, don't you?" she said. "You can defend me if need be, can you not?"

"Well, yes."

"And as for becoming lost—look, this is a well-worn trail. More so than I remember it, really. Last I came here it was quite overgrown."

"Still. I will have to answer to your mother if I keep you out after dark."

"A spring dampens the path here," she warned. "Take care, the ground is slippery." She took her own advice, stepping carefully through the slick white clay. The chapel rose ahead, caught in a low beam of westering light that sifted through the trees. She found a pleasant view and stopped to admire it, leaning against the husky bole of a palm.

Even in its age and disrepair she thought the chapel was beautiful. Built of white stone, its every surface was figured with serpents, flowers, dancing figures, and symbols of air and night.

"Lovely, isn't it?" she said. "In their day, the Tamanja built magnificent things. Before the Drehhu destroyed their civilization."

"There's not so much to them now," Lucien said. "Passable

laborers, but of little use in any higher capacity. They are lucky to have our protection."

"Yes," she said. "Our protection."

"I admit, though, that it's a fetching sight," Lucien said. "May I now escort you home?"

"You know," Chrysanthe said, "there is a ghost here. If you stand just in this place, sometimes she makes herself known." She took a few steps toward the chapel and then stopped. Took a deep, slow breath as Lucien joined her. "You feel that?" she whispered. "Like water running across your face?"

"I—yes!" Lucien said. "That is quite amazing."

Chrysanthe smiled. She had been only eight when she discovered the ghost.

"Close your eyes," she said, shutting hers. For a moment, there was nothing but darkness, but then a face formed, a girl's face with broad cheekbones and green eyes.

Mah simki? Simi Sasani, a voice murmured.

"Oh!" Lucien said. Chrysanthe opened her eyes and saw that he had jumped back a yard.

"Were you startled?" she asked. "I did warn you."

"It's just… your voice sounded so strange. Not like you at all."

"Oh, did I speak?" Chrysanthe asked.

"Yes, in some strange language."

"That was *her*," she said. "The ghost. The language is an antique form of Tamanja. She asked my name and said hers was Lotus."

"I did not hear a ghost speak, only you."

She nodded. "I am sensitive to ghosts," she replied. "I always have been, like my grandmother was. Parfait Hazhasa at the basilica says it's not common, but not unheard of either."

"I see." Lucien nodded. "How terribly interesting. Now may I renew my offer to walk you home?" He still seemed agitated.

"That's agreeable," she said, and watched the relief spread on his face.

"Wait a moment," she said. "Do you hear something?"

"Another ghost?" he asked.

"No. In the chapel."

"No," he replied. "Nothing."

"Let's have a look."

"Chrysanthe!" he said sharply. "If someone is there, they might well be thieves or vagabonds."

"Well, if so, they have no right to take up residence on my father's estates," she said. "You have your sword. We shall investigate."

"You are far too rash," he complained.

But he followed as she crept toward the chapel. The building's base was oval, some forty feet in length, with an entrance on the east side. Before they had reached the opening, a man stepped out. He was a rough-looking fellow, dressed in worn cotton shirt and pants. His lips were bisected by a scar that resembled a white caterpillar when he closed his mouth. He had a short, heavy sword thrust in his belt.

He glared at the two of them.

"What is this?" he demanded.

"What are you doing in there?" she demanded. "I am Chrysanthe Nevelon. These are Nevelon holdings. Step aside, please." Beside her, Lucien drew his sword.

"Do as she says."

Reluctantly, the man moved away from the door. Chrysanthe approached the chapel and looked within. The fearful, wide-eyed gazes of some fifteen children looked back at her. They were dirty, clad in rags, and bound together by chains.

"Danesele!" one of them cried.

"Yes, Eram," she said. "We shall have this all fixed, very soon."

She turned back to Lucien, who now stood with the other man, facing her.

"Chrysanthe…" he began. His sword did not quite threaten her, but aimed at some point between her feet and his.

"I do not like coincidences, Lucien," she told him. "True happenstance is vanishing rare. The children began disappearing soon after you arrived. I inquired about and discovered that you had made some odd purchases—chains, for instance—and I once noticed a bluish-black stain on your kerchief. It looked like ahzha, which is often used by slavers to pacify their victims.

"At times," she continued, "you had on your coat a scent of burnt dung, which is what the villagers use for fuel. *What business would you have in the villages?* I wondered. In time, my only question became where you were keeping your prey until you could move them to the trade, and then I noticed the white clay on your boots. This is the only place I know of where that particular color of soil is present.

"And you." She nodded at the other man. "I recognize you. You work for my father. How could you betray him so?"

Lucien looked terrified, his features working.

"Chrysanthe," he said. "This all can be explained—"

"Yes," she said. "The explanation is that you're selling into slavery children under my father's protection."

"They are little better than slaves as it is," he said, starting to look angry.

"That is not true," she said. "They are paid wages, and they may not be purchased or sold."

"Accidents happen," the other man suddenly said. "There is a place, not far from here. Many crocodiles. She went out alone, she never comes back…"

Lucien pursed his lips and broke eye contact. He looked like a trapped civet.

"Lucien," Chrysanthe said. "There are two reasons I did not let you kiss me. The first, I think you now know. The second reason is that if my brothers saw you taking such liberties with me, they might kill you."

"Your brothers?" he said. "They were not there."

"Oh, Lucien," she said. "Of course they were."

Lucien paled and turned as her eldest brother Tycho emerged from the trees. At twenty-four he was six years her senior, as brown-skinned as their father. Like her, his hair fell in curls to his shoulders, although in his case the locks were almost ebony. He wore a hunting jacket and broad-brimmed straw hat that stood in marked contrast to Lucien's finery.

"Another of your games played out, sister?"

Upon his arrival, Lucien's partner in crime suddenly bolted toward the jungle deeps, only to be arrested at sword-point by Gabrien, the next eldest, his cropped red-gold hair like a mirror of the drowning sun. He had their mother's thin, fine nose, which along with his coloring—and certain behaviors—had earned him the nickname Li Goupil, or "the Fox." Theron—the youngest at fifteen—came close behind, a bow and six arrows couched casually in one hand. Theron and Chrysanthe shared the same heart-shaped face, deep brown complexion, and blonde hair. Despite the age difference, people often thought them twins.

Lucien spun and sprang toward her, his expression fervid. She had almost been expecting something like that and had quietly slipped a bodkin into her hand, but her shoes were still slippery from the mud and she slid on the ancient limestone of the chapel. She dropped her knife and, before she could find her balance, Lucien grabbed her.

"Listen," he cried. "I mean none of you any harm. I only intended to earn a bit of profit."

"You took a walk off that road," Tycho said, "when you put hands on my sister." He laid his hand on the grip of his saber.

"Stepping into a big crack," Theron confirmed, laying an arrow on his bowstring.

"Maybe we should visit those oh-so-convenient crocodiles," Gabrien suggested.

"No, *listen*," Lucien pleaded, desperately. His sword was at her throat; she could feel the edge nicking her. "You three back off. I only want to reach the emperor's consul and assure my survival from you… barbarians."

"All of this sweet talk," Gabrien said. "You're right, Santh, quite a romantic fellow."

"Lucien," Chrysanthe said. "Listen to me quite carefully. The penalty for kidnapping children is something your family will be able to pay off, in time, but if you hurt me—Lord forbid that you should kill me—there will be no court for you. You will be hacked to pieces, and your head put on a spike so the vultures can peck it to the bone."

He seemed to sag, but the sword did not waver.

"They will kill me anyway," he said. He was weeping.

"I will ask them not to."

He tightened his grip. "Why should…?" he began, but then a

hand appeared in front of her face, coming from behind. It grabbed the blade at her throat and pushed it away. Lucien yelped and let her go. She stumbled back against the chapel as someone slammed Lucien to the ground, following him down.

No, not someone. Two men, in the sable-and-aubergine uniforms of the Emperor's Navy. Lucien tried to fight back to his feet, but one of the men dealt him a terrific blow to the chin. The other fellow picked himself up and stood aside, throwing her a concerned look with his wide blue eyes.

"Crespin!" she shouted. "Oh, Crespin!"

Her brother's companion, a lanky fellow with unruly brown hair spilling from beneath a seaman's cap, kicked Lucien in the ribs.

"Miserable excuse for a dog!" he shouted. "Shit from a bastard hyena…"

"Renost!" she cautioned. "Do not kill him."

Renost kicked the man again. "I'm not your brother," he said. "I'm not bound by your request."

"We need him, Renost," she insisted. "To find the other children."

Renost stood there, panting heavily for a moment, his black eyes blazing. Then he nodded.

"But for the grace of her," he told the moaning Lucien, then he spit on him. Crespin had reached her by then, and she threw her arms around him.

"We were bringing you a little surprise when Theron reported that you had wandered off with this fellow," Tycho said, nodding at Lucien. "I suppose it's a bit more of a surprise now."

"It is," she said. "Of course it is. A wonderful surprise. Crespin, I thought you had another year at sea before we would see you again. And you, Renost…"

She suddenly realized Renost was bleeding heavily from one hand. It must have been he who had grabbed Lucien's sword.

"That?" he grunted, noticing her attention. "Just a nick." Then his eyes went wide, and he fumbled to remove his hat. "Danesele," he said.

"Travel has made you more presentable, Renost," she said, "but formal address is unnecessary. Despite your protests, you are as much a brother to me as these others." It was then she noticed a third fellow in the emperor's colors, a nice-looking young man with straw-colored hair watching everything with what she took to be surprised amusement.

"Sir," she said, nodding.

"Oh, sister," Crespin said. "I am remiss. This is our companion, the most excellent seigneur Hector de la Forest, our ship's surgeon. He came ashore with us at our urging, so he might see for himself that our country is not so savage as he has heard."

"I am most pleased to meet you," Forest said, making a little bow. "And to you, Crespin, I must apologize for my former opinion. Not a jot of savagery to be seen here. But perhaps our friend Renost could use a bit of aid?"

Renost shrugged. Blood continued to pour from his hand.

"Really," Chrysanthe said. "Let's wrap that up." She ran her gaze over the whimpering, supine form of Lucien, and his accomplice, who—despite his sun-darkened face—seemed as pale as a cotton boll.

"Unchain these children," she told him.

"Yes, lady," he said.

"Theron," Tycho said, "fetch the horses." He turned to Chrysanthe. "We'll see to them," he said. "Crespin and Renost will escort you back home." She checked an objection—she wanted to see the children returned, but who knew how long Crespin would be in port.

"Thank you, Tycho," she said. "And you two," she added to Theron and Gabrien. "Where would I be without you?"

"Crocodile food, I reckon," Gabrien said.

NIGHT FELL softly, stirred by warm winds fragrant with the perfumes of orchids and water lilies. Beyond the terrace, fireflies danced above the swollen waters of the Laham River as bright Hesperus set into the trees and lesser stars brightened. A night bird trilled, accompanied by the strains of a harp. Chrysanthe glanced over at Forest, who was gazing out over the river.

"I'm sorry for your rude introduction to our country, seigneur de la Forest."

"Eye-opening to be sure," he said, "but I've spent some time in company with your brother, so these events are perhaps not so surprising." He swept his glass around. "And this is all so lovely," he said. "You are all so gracious to invite me to your home."

"Where do you call home, seigneur?"

"Please, call me Hector," he replied. "My home is a little-known place, I'm afraid. Poluulos."

"The island in the Mesogeios Sea?" she said. "Known for its excellent timber?"

"You astonish me," Forest said. He looked over at Crespin. "Your sister astonishes me."

"Oh, yes," Crespin said. "We are all quite astonished."

Forest looked back to her and nodded. "Yes, that is indeed the place. In fact, its timber was once so excellent that, at present, not a single tree remains on that little rock."

"That, I was not aware of," Chrysanthe said.

Hector spread his hands. "Well," he said, "the timber is gone, but we still have young boys in plenty to grow up and go into the emperor's service, and so here I am, in this very excellent company. Tell me, Danesele, is your life always so exciting as it was today?"

"Yes," Renost answered. "Because she makes it so."

"Exactly," Crespin said. "You realize, Chrysanthe, that eventually one these escapades of yours will end... badly."

"It did end badly, for Lucien," Tycho pointed out, taking his seat. He had traded his hunting attire for a zawb, the loose linen robe favored by the native Tamanja. The younger boys were still cleaning up.

"I mean for her," Crespin said. "And she knows it."

"I cannot stand idly by while my father is robbed or his reputation compromised," she protested.

"Tycho is in charge when Father is away," Crespin replied. "He is fully capable of seeing after the business. It's not like when were children, pretending to be agents of the empire—"

"Remember that secret language you two used to scribble in?" Renost said.

"It wasn't a language," Chrysanthe said. "It was a cypher." She shot a mock frown at her brother. "Did you come all and across the sea just to lecture me, dear brother?"

Crespin spread his hands. "The lecture is done," he said. "I only urge you to exercise some sense."

"Like you, I suppose?" she said. "Renost, Hector, tell me truthfully. Has my brother stayed clear of trouble during his time in the Navy?"

Renost grinned. "Well, that all depends on what you mean by trouble."

"Renost!" Crespin said.

"Is it trouble, for instance, to offend the Veil of Codaey by offering his daughter inappropriate gifts?"

"Flowers!" Crespin protested.

"Red jonquines, to be particular," Renost said. "They have a very specific symbolism in Codaey. Shall I explain?"

"No need," Chrysanthe said hastily, glancing at her younger sister Phoebe, whom she found gazing at Renost with adoring eyes. When the girl noticed Chrysanthe watching her, she quickly returned her regard back to her harp strings.

"I was innocent of their meaning," Crespin alleged.

"Was it trouble to climb upon the roof of the holy sepulcher of Phejen?" Renost went on. "Trouble only for the city watch, who pursued him throughout the town for the better part of the night."

"Us," Crespin amended, waving a finger between them. "Pursued *us*."

Renost raised his wine. "Well," he allowed, "It was an excellent view." The two men clinked their glasses together.

"I see," Chrysanthe said. "So I'm to be advised against a little housecleaning, while you two leave every port in shambles?"

Crespin frowned. "Is this true?" he asked Renost. "Every port?"

"No," Hector said. "The two of you left Isle Saint in good order. Hardly touched."

"There," Crespin said. "You overstate the case, sister."

"*Trop*, enough!" Chrysanthe said. "No more of your mishaps, but tell me this—what happy chance brings you home to us early?"

Crespin's squared features settled into more serious lines. "The same turn of fate that will bring Father back home tomorrow, or the next."

The harp stopped abruptly.

"Father returns?" Phoebe gasped.

"He does," Crespin replied.

"We shall all be together, then!" Phoebe said joyfully. At fifteen, her capacity for mercurial elation—and misery—seemed boundless.

"For a time," Crespin said.

Chrysanthe felt a sudden worry creep into her ear and down to her throat.

"What is it, Crespin?"

"War," he replied. "We are going to war."

Silence fell for a moment. Chrysanthe was considering what to say when the door burst open behind her.

"Chrysanthe!" her mother bellowed. "What have you done?"

CHAPTER THREE

HOUND

THE VALLEY OF ELMEKIJE

1014 E.N.

AS HE watched the baron's horsemen gallop down below, Hound was suddenly sorry he'd done such a good job in laying the false trail. They had fallen for it and were going the wrong way—the chase was over before it had begun. The idiots were only yards away, but they would never see him, hidden as he was in the leafy stand of hog-laurels.

That can be fixed, he thought.

With a wild shout, he bounded down the hill and flung himself at the rearmost horseman. With the back of his tomahawk, he rang the fellow's helmet like a bell. Before the rider had toppled from his saddle and slammed heavily to earth, Hound was already hurtling up the hill on the other side of the path.

"He's there!" one of the men shouted.

Belatedly a few arrows hissed through the oaks, none very close to him. He whooped mockingly as he once again vanished from their sight, then chuckled at the litany of curses that followed.

Running along the ridge top for a few paces, he descended into the next valley in long leaps that sent him skidding on leaf mold. It felt almost as if he was flying. The curses were still there, and the crashing of horses and armored men through the undergrowth.

Hound was not so encumbered—he wore nothing but a loincloth and a belt that supported his small ax and a bag of smooth stones.

He vaulted over the stream at the base of the valley, ran a few more steps, and then stopped in front of a wall of thorny briars. Putting his ax back in his belt, he took one of the pebbles from his bag and appraised it before uncoiling the sling from his wrist. Then he fitted the stone into the elk-hide pocket.

The men came down the hill now. One of them, named Detel—a burly fellow with red hair—spotted him.

"Shoot!" Detel bellowed. A few more arrows came his way, this time with better aim, and Hound stepped behind a sweetgum.

"You little piece of govno," Detel shouted. "Today is the end of you."

"Well, everyone has their day," Hound yelled back. He stuck his head out from behind the trunk. "But tell me—what are you fellows so mad about?" He ducked back as a feathered shaft thunked into the tree.

"Trespass in my lord's forest," the man responded. "Every kind of petty thievery. Vandalism. Witchery. Chicken stealing—"

"I think you covered chickens under petty thievery," Hound shot back. "Yes?"

"Get him!" Detel roared.

Hound took the time to pick out the best of the archers. Whirling his sling, he stepped from behind the tree. The man wore a helmet with a nose guard, so Hound sent the missile into his unprotected throat. Then he flung himself into the briars, dropping down on hands and knees to scuttle along the slightly less congested forest floor.

He emerged from the thorns at the edge of a cliff which dropped about twice the height of his body down to a beaver pond. He jumped and hit the deepest part. Surfacing, he swam to shore. From there, he turned east and began to work his way back behind his pursuers, reckoning there might be some fun yet to be had with them.

He checked the sky, saw a raven circling, and smiled.

Climbing a huge magnolia, he perched in the upper branches and watched the first of the baron's knights hack his way through the briars, lose his balance, and topple into the beaver pond. Another man emerged: Hound gauged the distance. They were just at the edge of his range, so chances were another stone would only alert them to his location. Which might be fun—starting the chase up again—but probably wouldn't be. Better he return to Grandmother to tell her what he had seen.

He was starting down the almost ladder-like arrangement of limbs when he heard a twig snap. Looking down, he found himself facing the point of an arrow on a drawn bow. Wielding the bow was a lean man with surprisingly blue eyes and not much hair. He stood in a copse of fern trees nearly as tall as he was. A pack rested on the ground not far from his feet.

"Easy, there," the man said in Velesan, but with an accent that sounded as if he was from someplace east. "They'll pay me more for you alive than dead."

"Course they would—that goes without saying."

"So drop your chopper down, the sling and the stones."

"Let me think on that," Hound said.

"I can hit a bird on the wing," the man informed him. "I can put this shaft through an arm, and the next through your other."

He didn't sound like he was bragging.

"Hold off," Hound said, dropping his weapons to the fern-covered floor. The man kicked them away from the tree, never relinquishing his aim.

"Now come on down," he said.

"They hired you in from someplace, didn't they?" Hound said as he descended. "Kind of flattering. You're smart, too. Let them provide a distraction while, all along, you were tracking me."

"That's about right."

"You know they'll kill me," Hound said. "And for what? A bit of fun?"

"That's not for me to sort out," the man said. "I'm just doing what I'm paid for."

Hound settled his feet on the ground and faced the man.

"Toruti," Hound said.

"What?"

"A word in Kansa," Hound said. "It means 'attack'."

"Don't test—"

A massive red-brown shape bounded from the undergrowth and slammed the man to the ground. The bow whined and the arrow sighed off through the ferns.

"Wasn't talking to you," Hound said. "Talking to Rose." The man wasn't likely listening; the huge dog had him pinned with her forepaws on his shoulders and was yanking his head back and forth by way of his ear. Hound fetched his weapons, then picked up the man's bow and cut the string with his ax.

"Alright Rose," he said. "Let's not end him."

Rose looked up at him, a severed ear in her teeth. She kept the man pinned while Hound searched his pack. In it he found chains which had no doubt been meant for him.

The man started to scream for help.

"I can always have her take your throat out," Hound said.

The man stopped shouting and settled for groaning.

"My ear," he moaned.

"Give him his ear back, Rose," Hound said.

The dog dropped her bloody prize on the man's face. Then Hound chained him and hefted up the pack, reckoning there might be other things worth having. He heard a flutter of wings as Soot settled on his shoulder.

"There you are," he said to the raven. He nodded at the bound man. "You could have let me know about him." He turned and began to set off.

"You can't leave me here," the man said.

"Yeah," Hound said. "Yeah, I can, but look—those other fellows will be here in a rabbit's piss. You'll be fine."

"It's true what they told me," the man said. "I thought they were simple."

"What did they tell you?"

"That you're a witch, and consort with demons."

Hound blinked. "You mean Soot and Rose?" He pointed first at the raven, and then the dog.

"Demons."

"Yep," Hound said, "and you can spread that around, if you want." Then he left, quickly. The baron's men were stupid, but not deaf.

HE COULD always feel it when he entered Grandmother's forest, never mind which direction he came in from. There was just something different about the air, the light, the way everything seemed to lean slightly inward. Here was his cradle, his hearth, the center of his world.

Here he was safe.

It was the only home he remembered, but it was not where he was born—Grandmother found him as a baby, alone in the woods. She taught him to speak Kansa, to forage and hunt. As he grew older, he wandered the forests and grasslands of the valley, and later the hills and mountains around it. He found the village of Berze on the river Vlone and watched how other people lived. Eventually he was befriended by some of the bolder children in the village, and from them he learned Velesan, the language of the south.

For a time he traded in Berze, bringing pelts, mushrooms, honey, and such to exchange for iron tools, sweets, bread, and wine. During that time, he lived half in the world of men—until he took up with Leste, a girl also fancied by the son of the baron whose castle overshadowed the town. Then he was suddenly accused of all sorts of things—witchcraft, theft, hunting illegally in the baron's forest. Only the last of these was true, but it didn't matter. There had always been those who were suspicious of him, especially the elders. So, he was forbidden to approach the village.

Hound decided that if he was going to be accused of such things, he might as well do them, and began amusing himself at the baron's expense. When that grew boring and the wanderlust struck him, he would travel deep into the mountains and the villagers would begin to think he was dead or gone forever.

When he became weary of being alone, he returned to pilfer and vandalize, drive cattle into the woods, and play tricks on the baron's huntsmen and messengers—always to return to the safety of Grandmother's forest.

He followed along a little stream and soon reached her cave. It didn't seem like much from the outside—just an opening in a moss-covered hillside not much larger than the door of a house—but the roots of the cave went deep. *Very* deep, maybe to the bottom of the world. He had explored it a bit when he was younger, but preferred his adventures under the sky.

Grandmother was there, as always. Dressed in a homespun shift and shawl, she hunched near the fire he'd started that morning. Her hair was black today, with no sign of the gray from the day before, and her eyes were green rather than brown. She was never the same from one dawn to the next, Grandmother. Sometimes she didn't even look like a person. She once told him that for many years she hadn't worn any appearance at all, but had made the effort after he came along.

"Springling," she said. "How long have you been gone this time?"

"Only a part of a day," he said.

"It's hard to tell," she said. "A year, a day, the same to me."

"I know, Grandmother."

"But not for you," she said, fixing him with her emerald gaze. "How many winters have you seen?"

"Seventeen or eighteen," he replied. It was a conversation they had had before, fairly often. It was more or less her way of saying hello. He began unloading the pack, which he found contained some bread, a small skin of wine, a purse with ten silver Velesan korls, and a whetstone.

"Eighteen," grandmother said. "It must be eighteen. That's a long time for me to be awake." She smiled. "But I have enjoyed you, Springling."

"I love you too, Grandmother," he said, and he glanced up. "I saw strangers at the baron's castle this morning. I think they've been there for a few days. Two of the servants were talking, and one said they were from Ophion Magne, but no one was supposed to know that. She also said the baron was afraid of them." He returned his attention to the pack.

Grandmother nodded but didn't say anything.

"Where is Ophion?" he asked. "Is it far?"

"I don't know," she said. "The sound of the name is familiar. Someone I knew once, I think." Something about the way she said it arrested him. He looked away from the pack and back to her.

"Is something wrong?" he asked.

"You'll be gone soon."

"I go all the time," he said. "I always come back."

"No," she said. "Gone."

"You mean dead?" he asked. "What do you mean?"

She shook her head. "You will be gone by tomorrow."

CHAPTER FOUR

THE EMPEROR'S CALL

"HELLO, DEAR mother," Crespin said, standing. Renost also hastily rose to his feet, followed by Hector.

"Crespin?" she gasped. "Crespin?" She looked around accusingly. "Why did no one tell me my son has returned?" she demanded. "Why was this kept from me? We should have had a feast, a celebration."

"It was at my request, Mother." Crespin took a few steps, took their mother in his arms, and kissed her cheek. "I didn't want any fuss, most certainly not a party. And I wanted to surprise you."

"Well, you certainly have done that," she muttered. "Look at me."

Chrysanthe couldn't quite suppress an exasperated sigh. Iole Nevelon looked beautiful. She always did, and treated it as a duty to be so—although it was not difficult, given her natural gifts. The years had dulled the luster of her gilded tresses, but only a little, and her pale features were fine and regular. She was never seen uncoifed or in disarray, and yet here she was acting as if she were wearing a bloodstained swine-slaughtering apron rather than a gown of silk brocade.

Mother shifted her accusing gaze back to Chrysanthe.

"I haven't forgotten about you," she said. "And you boys. Lucien de Delphin is of noble blood, and you beat him half to death. Any prospects you ever had, Chrysanthe—"

"You must think low of me to believe I would consider such a man," Chrysanthe said.

"All men are animals," Ione said, "and they all can be tamed. The business you claim he was engaged in was unfortunate, but far from unforgivable."

"He put a sword to our sister's throat," Theron said, stepping into the room. "He's lucky to be alive."

"We'll see who is lucky when his complaint reaches the court," Ione replied. Then she waved the subject off with the back of her hand. "Enough of that. Introduce me to this young man."

Crespin did so, as Hector bowed. The two exchanged a few pleasantries before his mother returned her attention to him.

"What brings you home, Crespin?"

"War!" Phoebe blurted. "And Father returns as well."

"Alastor?" she said. "What war? Who attacks us?"

"It is we who are attacking, Mother," Crespin said. "The emperor has called us up: not just the Navy, but parts of the mercantile fleets, as well." He was silent for a moment; to Chrysanthe's immense surprise, her mother did not interject anything, but granted him the pause.

"We're to attack Basilisk," he finally said. "We will throw down the Basilisk Throne and have an end to the whole matter."

"Sacre merde," Gabrien swore.

"Gabrien," Ione snapped, but there was a bit of a quiver in her voice.

"Why?" Chrysanthe asked. "It's been years…"

"Four hundred and some quibbling," a new voice interrupted. Chrysanthe bounded to her feet in delight.

"Father!" she shouted.

Alastor Nevelon was trim, angular, and composed. He rarely moved unless with a particular purpose. His black hair was shot with gray, but his blue-green eyes shone like the shallows of the sea. A faint smile traced his lips.

"Husband!" Ione said. "You as well?" She glared at Crespin. "How cruel of you not to tell me!"

"I was coming around to it," Crespin said, "but I didn't know when he would arrive—I thought no earlier than tomorrow, to be honest. You had fair wind, Father."

"Passing," the older man replied. "I have a superior ship and an excellent crew to—"

He was interrupted by Phoebe hurling herself at him, and then the rest crowded around. Crespin, Chrysanthe noticed, hung back until last. The relationship between father and son had been uneasy for some time, and when Crespin entered the Imperial Navy rather than joining Father in the sugar trade, there had been some unpleasant words on both sides.

"Is it really war, Papa?" Phoebe asked as Alastor took a glass of wine from Tycho and settled onto a chair.

He nodded. "Four hundred years we've been fighting the Drehhu. When the first fleets found this place, those creatures had already conquered most of the world. I need not remind anyone of their depredations, the horrors our forefathers discovered when they liberated the slaves. The horrors I..."

He stopped, frowned and took a sip of his wine. A profound silence followed his unfinished statement, and they all knew why.

Alastor Nevelon, her father, had been captured at the battle of the Expiry and had been enslaved by the Drehhu for three years before making his escape and returning to the land of his birth. It was not something he usually mentioned.

Finally, he cleared his throat and continued.

"For all these centuries we've pushed them back, inch by bloody inch, until only Basilisk remains."

"Only?" Tycho said skeptically. "They may no longer possess an empire, but they still have more than enough of their demon ships and weapons to defend their city. The last fleet that tested them was crushed."

"That was then," Alastor said.

"How are things different?" Chrysanthe asked.

"In three ways," her father said. "The first is that they are weaker. Their fortresses at Escepel and Triey are out of their hands. The second is that the Cryptarchia has agreed to supply each of our ships with a strixe, even for those who cannot pay the guild tax. Finally, Ophion does not venture this alone. Fleets from Velesa and Modjal will join us."

"Also," Renost added, "the last time Basilisk was attempted, Crespin, Hector, and I were not involved." He smiled and held up his wineglass, but Chrysanthe noticed that Crespin was fighting a frown. He was so like Father at times, trying to shelter behind an emotionless mask—but he wasn't nearly so successful at it.

"It sounds *glorious*," Phoebe said.

"You won't think so if Father or Crespin or Renost here comes back on his shield," Chrysanthe said. "Why? Why *now*?"

Alastor took another drink of his wine.

"It is not for us to debate," he said. "The emperor has called for us, and we shall go."

"The emperor didn't call me," Crespin said. "I was already in his service."

"So you were," Alastor replied, and Chrysanthe saw there was something there, something new and raw between them. But her father did not acknowledge it further. "Tycho," he said instead. "Tell me how things are coming along. The new fields, back along the river?"

"Some ticks to work out," Tycho said. "Nothing serious or interesting. You might ask Chrysanthe about her latest adventure, however."

As her father turned toward her, his face stern, she felt her cheeks reddening.

"Adventure?" he said. "I thought we had discussed these 'adventures'."

Chrysanthe reached for her wineglass.

"Not so much discussed," she replied, "as negotiated—and negotiations need have no end, but can eternally…" She trailed off as his head tilted a little.

She knew the look.

"Well," she said, after a drink and a deep breath. "You should know. It was about Lucien, you see…"

THE NEXT morning, Chrysanthe found Phoebe in the parlor, lying on a rug with a large book spread open before her. She bent over her sister's shoulder to have a look. The pages were turned to a depiction of a waterway hedged on either side by massive cliffs. At the base of each cliff stood gigantic metal statues, manlike but not men. Their arms and legs were both a bit too long, their shoulders far too broad.

"Anvvod," Phoebe said, "and the Colossus Gate."

While at first glance some thought Chrysanthe and Theron were twins, Phoebe actually *was* Theron's twin. But they did not look alike. Her brown hair had hints of copper in it, and her face was close to round.

Chrysanthe tapped the image of one of the metal statues.

"The colossi aren't there anymore," she said. "They were destroyed a hundred years ago."

"I know," Phoebe said. "Heron l'Archier defeated them."

"I think the two hundred ships he had with him might have helped him a little," she said dryly. "Contrary to what your books say, it is rare for an admiral to leave his command and attack the foe single-handedly."

Phoebe frowned. "In *Li Romanz de Heron*…"

"That is fiction," Chrysanthe said. "You must learn to distinguish between fiction and history."

"History is dull."

"The actual Battle of the Colossus Gate was anything but dull," Chrysanthe said. "Hundreds of ships were destroyed. Thousands died, and when it was over, Basilisk still stood."

"But the colossi were demolished," Phoebe insisted. "Father and Crespin will not have to face them, at least." When her sister clung to a concept, she stubbornly refused to loosen her grip, even a little. Chrysanthe continued.

"No, but they will need to confront weapons that fling fire and iron, black sorcery and diabolic ships—and after that, the walls of the fortress itself."

"The Drehhu are an evil which must be defeated," Phoebe insisted. "I'm proud that Father and Crespin and… Renost… are going to battle against them."

Chrysanthe sighed, rose, and pulled another book from the shelves. She lay down on the floor next to Phoebe and opened it to the map in the center.

"The Drehhu Empire," she said. "Four centuries ago. It comprised most of the world, as you can see."

"I know that."

"Here, here, and here," she went on, "in what is now outermost Ophion, Velesa, and Modjal. The ends of the world, and the only lands that were free of the Drehhu Empire."

"And the Christ of Ophion made a miracle," Phoebe said, "and sent the fleets."

"It may have been Christ Ophion," Chrysanthe allowed. "Some older texts suggest it was a conjuring by the elder Cryptarchia, but yes, the fleets arrived, mariniers from elsewhere. With the people of the ends of the world, they pushed against the margins of the Drehhu Empire. In time, they won more territory. The Accord was reached, and Ophion, Modjal, and Velesa foreswore any aggression toward one another. Where they took land from the Drehhu, they made colonies. They divided the world up amongst themselves, all overseen by the Cryptarchia, which owes no allegiance to any single government but wields power in all of them.

"Our own province of Mesembria was liberated no more than a hundred years ago," she continued, "and was judged to become part of Ophion. Our ancestor, Orion Nevelon, was granted a charter by the Emperor Alexandros I for his service in that liberation, and so here we are."

"Why are you telling me all this?" Phoebe asked, a little petulantly. "I know it already."

Chrysanthe flipped forward in the book, to another map.

"Now we have three empires," she said. "Ophion, Modjal, and Velesa. Each with colonies spread around the world, and each of these empires has slavery, just as the Drehhu do."

"We don't own slaves," Phoebe said.

"Because Father, having been enslaved, abhors that institution. He formed the Mesembrian Mercantile Alliance, which follows the belief that free workers who have an interest in their business work harder and better at their trades. Yet Ophion does not forbid slavery, nor do either of the other two empires. We *could* own slaves, if we were so inclined."

"Are you trying to suggest that we're as bad as the Drehhu?" Phoebe asked, a hostile note in her voice.

"Not as bad," Chrysanthe replied, "but maybe not so much better." She traced her hands across the map. "Sugar, rum, and cotton move from Mesembria north and east to ports in mother Ophion, and then east to through the inland seas to Velesa and back south to Savor in the Modjal empire. Timber and furs ship down the through the Mer de Typhon from Velesa. Spices, precious stones, silk—these things come to us from the port of Savor. But most of what is traded there does not come from Modjal. It comes from further east, from Eosian lands, and the only way to go there by ship is through here."

She tapped the east side of the map, which was mostly void of detail. It showed a long peninsula arcing from Modjal to the south and east, where it almost joined with the larger mass of Timur. All along the narrow strip of land volcanoes were depicted, belching smoke and flame.

"The Salamandra," she said.

"I know all of this," Phoebe said. "To reach Basilisk one must brave burning mountains and treacherous reefs, and—"

"My point is," Chrysanthe interrupted, "that Basilisk and its fleet guards the only place a ship might pass through, and so the easternmost lands are denied us, at least by sea. We must rely on the Drehhu, and thus we must pay their tariffs."

Phoebe peered at the map more closely.

"Why not sail further south and pass around Timor?"

"That is precisely what the fleet tried, when Father sailed with it," Chrysanthe said. "They hoped to come at Basilisk from the east, where they would not be expected, but it is an exceptionally long trip, much further than if one could pass through the strait in the Salamandra. And there is this." She tapped the edge of the map.

"Oh," Phoebe said. "The Expiry."

"Yes. To go that way requires an awfully close approach to the Expiry."

"And nothing that crosses into the Expiry ever comes back out."

"That is true," Chrysanthe said. "More than half of the ships in that ill-fated fleet passed into it and were never seen again. All of the survivors of the battle were enslaved, including Father." She shuddered inwardly, knowing how the experience had affected her father, the strongest man she had ever known.

"And yet you still insist the Drehhu are not evil?"

"That's not the point," Chrysanthe replied. "I'm saying this war isn't happening just because the Drehhu are evil. It's happening because trade is the lifeblood of our civilization, and Basilisk restricts it. For us, here in Mesembria, you might say the war is about the cost of sugar."

"Very cynically put," a voice said from the door.

Phoebe looked back over her shoulder and her cheeks darkened.

"Renost!" she said, embarrassed, climbing to her feet, patting at her dress so as not to show her legs. Chrysanthe rolled up to her knees and stood. "You should have knocked," Phoebe said. "You've caught us all disheveled."

"The door was open," Renost said. "And what's this sudden

modesty? I remember you hanging upside down from tree branches, not so long ago."

"I was a girl then!" Phoebe protested. "I am a woman now, if you hadn't noticed."

"And a most beautiful young woman," Renost agreed.

Phoebe blushed again. "You ought not to say things like that, Renost," she said. "It isn't proper." She squirmed a bit. "Although it would not be out of line if you were to… with mother's permission of course… coffee—" Phoebe suddenly covered her face with her hands. Then, with a little sob, she fled from the room.

"What in the world is wrong with her?" Renost asked.

"I think you are not so innocent that you do not know," Chrysanthe said.

His head dropped a little. "I think you overestimate my instincts in that area."

"Hmm," she replied, a bit doubtfully. "How is your hand?"

"Nothing serious," he said.

"I wish you had not injured yourself on account of my poor judgment," she told him.

"I couldn't have done otherwise," he said. Then he stood there, fidgeting for a moment. It was strange, and utterly uncharacteristic of him. As if she made him nervous, which was impossible, of course. They had grown up together.

"Do you remember the time," he finally said, "when we pretended you, Crespin, and I were Tritos, Akhos, and Parthenia? And we captured the Great Bull back from Ilion?"

She smiled at the memory. "As I recall, the Great Bull was portrayed by Dionysus, my pet pig."

"*Right*," he said, too quickly. "You remember, and afterward—"

Chrysanthe heard wind chimes in the courtyard and smelled ginger cake baking in the cookhouse. The sunlight coming through the window grew brighter as a cloud passed. In the corner of the room, at the ceiling, a cottage spider was taking down a web.

"Stop," she said softly. "I remember. The pretend wedding. Renost—"

"It was not pretend for me," he said softly. "Nor is it now."

"I know," she said, "but Renost, we were children. Such affection is encouraged in the young. In adults, it is not—and Crespin has determined to be an adult."

"You've known this all along?" he said.

"Of course."

"And does *he* know?"

"If he does, he will not admit it to himself," she said. "He loves you."

"But not in that way."

"Even if he did, it would not matter," she said. "He will do what it expected of him. He will take a wife and father children."

"You seem in no rush to marry."

"Indeed," she said. "I am not. Perhaps I *will* not."

"It is expected of you," he said.

"Of course," she replied, "but I am not my brother, Renost. Why do you bring this up now?"

"I thought you could advise me," he said. "I feel I should confess to him."

"Because you're going to war? You've been in battle before."

"I fear this shall be different."

"I hope it shall not be," she replied. "But if you truly ask my counsel—do not do this. The outcome will not be to your liking, and it may damage your friendship."

He nodded. "That is what I feared you would say."

———

"WHAT'S THE matter with you, Renost?" Crespin asked, accepting the rum bottle from his sullen friend and taking a long drink before passing it along to Hector.

The three men sat on a broken crate in the factory district, between the massive yellow brick warehouses and the docks. They weren't alone in doing so. Barilors—weather-beaten, gnarled old men—clustered on barrels, boxes, and small heaps of brick. They sat drinking rum from ceramic pitchers, talking, playing eshecs and generally laying about. Most were pensioners from the Navy or merchant fleets. As boys, Crespin and Renost had come here to listen to them tell tall tales of their lives at sea. They had taken to calling each other mon vieil—"my old man"—in imitation of the barilors.

After a year in strange ports it felt… comfortable.

"It's nothing," Renost said. "An ill humor. It will pass."

"I hope so," Crespin said, taking the rum back from Hector. "There's nothing worse than a morose drunk."

"Very well said," Renost replied. "I shall brighten up, then." He nodded toward their ship, the *Pelerin,* a sturdy, six-masted vessel with portals for sweeps. "All too soon we'll be at sea again."

"Yes," Crespin said, "but not on that ship. Not me, at least."

"What do you mean?" Renost said. "You're third officer."

"I was," he replied. "Now I'm on the *Leucothea.*"

"Your father's ship?" Renost said. "It's not even a naval vessel."

"It is now. They've made my father an admiral for this little adventure, and he wants me on his ship. No one seems to care what I want."

"What *do* you want?"

"I want to stay with the *Pelerin* and my crewmates," Crespin said.

"I want to fight with the Navy, not deliver supplies."

"The mercantile fleets are outfitted to fight, as I understand it," Hector said. "They have quilaines, and each has a strixe on board."

"Yes, should we encounter danger on the voyage, we can put up a fight. Should every last ship of the Navy be lost, perhaps we will exchange fire with the Drehhu. And these strixes—they are so new, unproven. How much help will they be, really?"

"The Cryptarchia has employed them for years," Hector said.

"And how many wars have *they* fought?" Crespin asked.

Hector shrugged. "Leave that aside. A fleet fights on its belly as much as anything else. Relieved of carrying so much food and extra munitions, the Navy can pack its ships with more fighters. The mercantile fleet is key to our victory. Should it not arrive, the Navy will find itself starved and without shot for their quilaines."

"That's all true, I'm certain," Crespin said, "but it's not where I want to be."

"Perhaps the emperor gives no never-mind where you want to be," Renost said.

"It's not the emperor made this decision," Crespin said. "It was my father… and why this peevish tone? Are you glad we are to be separated?"

Renost frowned, then shook his head. "No," he murmured. "I had assumed we would sail together. But—"

"Well, about that," Crespin interrupted. "If you want to come with me, it can be arranged."

Renost blinked, and then slowly a smile lifted his face. "Of course, mon vieil." He slapped Crespin on the back and his mood seemed to improve.

"I'm relieved," Crespin said. "I was starting to worry I would have to die alone. He glanced apologetically at Hector. "I could put in a word with my father for you, as well."

"There's no need," Hector said. "Your father was short a surgeon. On the *Pelerin* I was lieutenant, but on the *Leucothea* I shall be chief."

"A promotion," Renost said. "Well done. No wonder you had such pretty words about the mercantile fleet."

"Yes," Hector said. "And so we shall all die together, Crespin."

"Yes,'" Renost said. "No thanks to our damn surgeon."

would be as vulnerable as naked children.

The three were armed with long spears and swords. Most of the other men were clothed in quilted leathers, and they had crossbows as well as swords. They had with them one woman, dressed much as the men except that her black quilted hauberk dropped below her knees like a dress. Beneath that she wore dark red leggings. She and one man stood a little apart from the rest. This man wore plain traveling clothes and a leather cap.

Hound considered what to do. Grandmother seemed to think these people had come for him, but why? She had been unclear about what she meant about him being "gone." He loved her, but also knew that she was used to things dying.

Would she send him to his death?

He didn't know, but she'd said he still would be safe here. To his knowledge, she had never actually lied to him.

"Down there," he shouted. "What is it you want?"

It was almost comical how all their heads turned his way at once. The plain-clad man stepped forward a few paces.

"Are you sent by Elmekije?" he asked. He spoke Velesan, but with an accent Hound did not recognize.

"I don't know anyone of that name," he replied. "Do you mean Grandmother?"

The man looked puzzled.

"You're the witch-boy the villagers talk of?" the woman asked. "The Hound?"

"It's just Hound," he said.

"Then it's you we're searching for," the man said.

"And why is that?" he asked. "Yesterday a stranger tried to snare me. Today more strangers arrive asking after me."

"The baron thought he could capture you and sell you to us," the man said. "We were not privy to the attempt until it was over. He has been… disciplined."

Hound's ears perked a bit at that. Who were these people who could "discipline" the baron?

"What do you want of me?"

"Doesn't it have to take your commands?" one of the men in armor said to the woman. "You summoned it, after all."

"No," she replied. "That isn't how it works. He must choose to go with us."

Go where? Hound almost said it aloud, but then he remembered Grandmother's map.

"You need a guide," he said. "To lead you to a certain peak in the Vereshalm Mountains."

"That is correct," the man in the cap said.

"And why should I do that?" Hound shot back.

"You will be paid," he said. "In coin, or whatever else we have to offer."

"I don't have much use for coin," he said. "Why do you want to go there?"

Before anyone could reply, the woman motioned for them to be silent. "I'm coming up to you," she said. "Don't be alarmed."

"Selene—" the man began.

"It will be fine, Martin."

Warily Hound watched her approach. He had never seen anyone like her. Her skin was so brown it was nearly black, and yet there was still something washed-out about her. Her face had a drawn and weary look. Pretty, though. Her eyes were almost black, but with golden flecks. Her hair, likewise, was mostly black, with a few strands of pale yellow.

She stopped a short distance away from him. He glanced at Rose, but the big dog seemed unconcerned.

"My name is Selene," she said. "Your name is really Hound?"

"Yes."

"Who named you?"

"I named myself, as a matter of fact."

She shrugged.

"Hound, I can't tell you why we're going there, but it is important, and we need you. And I promise you—it will not be dull."

He felt a sort of tug inside. In the back of his mind, he had always planned to venture further into those mountains, and it had been a long time since he had had been in the company of anyone besides Grandmother.

"Not dull, eh?" he said. "You mean dangerous."

"From what I've heard of you, that's no matter," she said, "I thought it would be insulting to say it to you."

He grinned a little.

"Will I get to see you naked?"

"No," she said without blinking.

"There's no bargaining on that point?"

"None."

He studied her strange eyes. He could go along for a while. If it got boring, he could always leave. Grandmother often said things that could be true in one way, and not in others. He could come back if he wanted, but maybe where they were going, he wouldn't *want* to come back. Maybe he *would* die.

It had to happen sometime.

"I won't ride one of those things," he said, gesturing at the horses. "I go on my own feet and at my own pace, and if this is some sort of trick, I'll kill all of you."

Her eyes widened slightly.

"We're not here to harm you or capture you," she said. "I swear to you. We *need* you."

"Another girl told me that once. She was lying."

Selene frowned. "I'm not a girl," she said. "And I'm not lying. You may not come back from this trip, but it won't be because we betrayed you. We all might die, for that matter. Without you—"

He held up his hand.

"You can stop now."

He turned and ran back to Grandmother's cave, but for the first time he could remember, she wasn't waiting to greet him. He entered, and she wasn't there.

"Grandmother?" he asked, then called, but she didn't answer. He had an odd clutching in his throat, and his eyes felt damp. A warm wind blew from the cave and seemed to wrap around him for a long moment. Then it, too, was gone.

Rose let out a strange, mournful wail.

Hound glanced once more around the only home he had ever known. Then, with a little shrug, he set about gathering a few things, placing them in the pack he had taken from the manhunter. When he went searching for warmer clothes, he found not the tatty buckskins he had worn on his last trip into the mountains, but a new shirt and long pants of supple elk-hide, embroidered with dark green serpentine coils.

"Thank you, Grandmother," he said as he placed the clothes into the pack. "And goodbye." Then he trotted back to where Selene and the men were preparing to leave, discouraged looks on their faces.

Selene's face brightened when he returned.

Seeing that was worth a day of his time, at least.

CHAPTER SIX

THE GATES OF CHANCE

ACCOMPANIED BY an escort—a guardsman named Chaur—Chrysanthe knocked lightly on the door of her father's office. He looked up from his papers and gestured for her to come in, waving for the escort to remain outside.

"Close the door behind you," he said.

She felt a flush of apprehension. Father had listened to her explanation of the business with Lucien, pretty much without comment. She had a feeling that the commentary was about to begin, but when she had settled onto the chair he indicated and she really had a chance to study his face, it wasn't what she expected. It didn't carry a stern or angry expression, but rather one of tenderness... and perhaps sorrow. It was almost shocking.

What could make his guard slip so?

"What's the matter, Papa?" she asked.

His mask snapped back into place, and he shook his head from side to side.

"Perceptive as always," he sighed.

"Is it about Lucien?"

"Yes, and no," he said. "Mind you, the man is a cur, and he got what he deserved. But it was unwise for you to be involved. You should have let Tycho handle it."

"I… I know," she said.

His left eyebrow lifted slightly.

"That must have been hard for you to say."

She nodded. "What trouble have I brought upon us?"

"It makes my decision so much harder," he said. She waited for him to explain, and after a moment of staring at nothing, he did.

"If I could choose one of my children—or anyone, for that matter—to tend to my affairs while I am away, I would choose you." He paused. "You must never tell Tycho this. He is a good man, and quite able to run the business, but you see things as others do not. You are headstrong, yet that can be trained into a useful quality."

"I don't understand," she said. "Is Tycho accompanying you to war?"

"No, he will remain here to see after things."

"Then why—"

"I am only expressing my regard for your intelligence," he said, a little brusquely, then he appeared to compose himself again. She sat back, thoroughly puzzled.

"Here is the matter," he continued. "In some few days, a ship will arrive from the capital. I shall by then already be at sea. The ship will remain here only long enough to take on a passenger, and that passenger will be one of my children."

He paused to let her absorb that.

"As a hostage," she murmured, feeling suddenly almost light-headed with understanding. "Of course."

He nodded. "The emperor does not make a man an admiral and put him in charge of a hundred ships without some assurance of that man's loyalty, now and in the future. So I must surrender one of my own to live in Ophion Magne until this business is concluded. Ordinarily I would send Theron, as he could benefit from an education in the capital. He would also stand less risk of running afoul of Lucien's family."

"You're letting them have me," she said.

"I am," he replied. "Because I need you there."

"I don't understand."

"This war," he replied. "There is something suspicious about the whole thing, something I can feel but the shape of which I cannot see. Only someone in the heart of it all has a chance to parse it out, and Theron... his qualities do not suit him for that task."

"You want me to be your spy?"

"In essence."

"In fact," she amended.

"Yes," he admitted. "In fact. You will not be imprisoned, or anything of the kind. It will be arranged for you to stay with one of your cousins—but it will not be without peril. Ophion is not like any place you have ever known. It is a nest of vipers, and if you step the wrong way, you will be bitten."

In that instant, the discussion seemed unreal—as was the fact that her father was willing to sacrifice her. For a moment her mind caught only on that, but then she recalled his expression when she first entered the room. She remembered that he and Crespin were going off to fight in a war from which they might not return. How could she not do her part?

"I am a Nevelon," she told. "I will do this."

"I never doubted that you would," he replied, but his tone had nothing of victory in it.

"My brothers will be trouble," she said, pushing on. "If you aren't here to curb them, they might—"

"Get themselves arrested or killed," he finished. "Yes, I know, and for that reason they must not be informed of this until you are gone. No one must."

She nodded.

"Supposing I discover something," she said. "How am I to communicate it to you?"

"That has also been arranged," he replied. He produced a silver box from his desk drawer and placed it in the on table. It was no longer than her index finger, half as wide, and had a hinged lid with a small clasp to keep it closed. "The means of communication are contained here," he said. "I shall explain to you how to use it, and you must keep this concealed. Tell no one of it—except one man. His name is Bonaventure, and you must contrive to meet him however you can."

She nodded.

"Good," her father said. He tapped the box.

"Now, as to this…"

CRESPIN SPENT several days exploring the ruts of his life. He visited old lovers and friends. With his brothers, he hunted spotted antelope in the deep forest, then drank with Renost until the first light of morning at The Lighthouse Tavern, and had a breakfast of sour wine and fried tripe at The Crocodile.

He road horseback with Chrysanthe alongside the lazy meander of the Laham river, and they picnicked beneath the fever trees on